Advance praise for *Text Complexity: Raising Rigor in Reading*

"Fisher, Frey, and Lapp offer an amazingly clear and succinct explanation of text complexity as identified by Common Core State Standards. They include a wealth of targeted examples for teacher modeling and engagement of students in collaborative reading tasks."

—*Page Dettmann, Executive Director of Middle Schools,*
Sarasota County School Board, Sarasota, Florida

"Provides expert advice for implementing a program designed to develop in all students the ability to read complex text. Features a thorough discussion of measuring and analyzing text complexity, matching readers with appropriate texts, and using research-based techniques to build in-depth comprehension of complex text. Discussions and explanations are enriched by examples that are both clear and compelling."

—*Thomas Gunning, Professor Emeritus, Southern Connecticut State University,*
and Adjunct Professor, Central Connecticut State University

"On a daily basis, teachers face the complex task of instructing their students to become critical and strategic readers. Once again, Doug Fisher, Nancy Frey, and Diane Lapp have developed a timely and wonderful resource to address a significant challenge all educators are grappling with through the implementation of the Common Core State Standards. This practical resource describes a number of factors teachers need to consider when determining the complexity of the texts their students are reading. The book provides instructional ideas and lessons that are user-friendly for teachers as they engage their students in tackling challenging text. The authors address many of the misconceptions related to engaging students with rigorous and challenging texts in the classroom. I believe the authors of this book have captured the true intent of Common Core Language Arts Standards, which, if implemented as effectively as described in this book, will lead to increased learning for all students!"

—*Carlene Lodermeier, Curriculum Coordinator for K–12 Literacy,*
Ankeny Community School District, Ankeny, Iowa

"'Close' reading of this text will reward educators with the most insightful, information-rich, and practical foundation and perspective on text complexity available to date. In the context of the Common Core State Standards for English/Language Arts, the authors provide (1) a masterful synthesis of traditional and more contemporary research exploring those factors in the text, the context, and the reader that contribute to the complexity of any text; and (2) substantive, practical instructional applications that will lead to the types of deep and consequential student engagements with texts for which educators have always strived."

—*Shane Templeton, Foundation Professor Emeritus of Literacy Studies, University of Nevada, Reno*

Text Complexity

Raising Rigor in Reading

Douglas Fisher
Nancy Frey
Diane Lapp

INTERNATIONAL
Reading Association
800 BARKSDALE ROAD, PO BOX 8139
NEWARK, DE 19714-8139, USA
www.reading.org

The International Reading Association attempts, through its publications, to provide a forum for a
wide spectrum of opinions on reading. This policy permits divergent viewpoints without implying
the endorsement of the Association.

Executive Editor, Publications   Shannon Fortner
Managing Editor   Christina M. Terranova
Editorial Associate   Wendy Logan
Design and Composition Manager   Anette Schuetz
Design and Composition Associate   Lisa Kochel

Project Editor   Renée Brosius

Cover   Design, Lise Holliker Dykes; Image, caliber_3D/Shutterstock.com

The publisher would appreciate notification where errors occur so that they may be corrected in
subsequent printings and/or editions.

Library of Congress Cataloging-in-Publication Data
Fisher, Douglas, 1965-
  Text complexity : raising rigor in reading / Douglas Fisher, Nancy
Frey, and Diane Lapp.
      p. cm.
  Includes bibliographical references and index.
  ISBN 978-0-87207-478-1
1. Reading comprehension. I. Frey, Nancy, 1959- II. Lapp, Diane. III.
Title.
  LB1573.7.F56 2012
  372.47--dc23

                    2012002488

Suggested APA Reference
Fisher, D., Frey, N., & Lapp, D. (2012). *Text complexity: Raising rigor in reading*. Newark, DE:
International Reading Association.

CONTENTS

Douglas Fisher, PhD, is a professor of education at San Diego State University (SDSU) and a teacher leader at Health Sciences High and Middle College in San Diego, California, USA. He received the Celebrate Literacy Award from the International Reading Association (IRA) and the Paul and Kate Farmer *English Journal* Writing Award from the National Council of Teachers of English and was a member of the SDSU teaching program that won the Christa McAuliffe Excellence in Teacher Education Award from the American Association of State Colleges and Universities in 2003. He has published numerous articles on reading and literacy, differentiated instruction, and curriculum design, as well as books, such as *Checking for Understanding: Formative Assessment Techniques for Your Classroom* (Association for Supervision and Curriculum Development [ASCD], 2007), *Better Learning Through Structured Teaching: A Framework for the Gradual Release of Responsibility* (ASCD, 2008), and *Enhancing RTI: How to Ensure Success With Effective Classroom Instruction and Intervention* (ASCD, 2010; all with Nancy) and *In a Reading State of Mind: Brain Research, Teacher Modeling, and Comprehension Instruction* (IRA, 2009) with Nancy and Diane. He can be reached at dfisher@mail.sdsu.edu.

Nancy Frey, PhD, is a professor of literacy in the School of Teacher Education at SDSU and a classroom teacher at Health Sciences High and Middle College. Before moving to San Diego, she was a special education teacher in the Broward County (FL) Public Schools, where she taught students at the elementary and middle school levels. With Doug, she was also a member of the SDSU teaching program that won the Christa McAuliffe Excellence in Teacher Education Award in 2003. Nancy has served as the chair of IRA's Print Media Award Committee. Her research interests include reading and literacy, assessment, intervention, and curriculum design, and she was a finalist for IRA's Outstanding

Dissertation of the Year Award. She has published in *The Reading Teacher,* *Journal of Adolescent & Adult Literacy, English Journal, Voices From the Middle, Middle School Journal, Remedial and Special Education, Educational Leadership,* and *California English.* She has coauthored books on literacy, such as *Improving Adolescent Literacy: Strategies at Work* (Allyn & Bacon, 2003), *Reading for Information in Elementary School: Content Literacy Strategies to Build Comprehension* (Allyn & Bacon, 2007), and *Scaffolded Writing Instruction: Teaching With a Gradual-Release Framework* (Scholastic, 2007; all with Doug). She teaches a variety of courses in SDSU's teacher-credentialing program on elementary and secondary reading instruction and literacy in content areas, classroom management, and supporting students with diverse learning needs. She can be reached at nfrey@mail.sdsu.edu.

 **Diane Lapp, EdD,** is the distinguished professor of education in the School of Teacher Education at SDSU, where she teaches preservice and graduate courses. She has taught in the elementary and middle grades and is currently an English/literacy teacher and a peer coach at the high school where she teaches. Her major areas of research and instruction cover issues related to struggling readers and writers who live in economically deprived settings, their families, and their teachers. Currently a coeditor of the National Council of Teachers of English's *Voices From the Middle* with Doug and Nancy, Diane has authored, coauthored, and edited many articles, columns, texts, handbooks, and children's materials on reading, language arts, and effective instructional issues. She has also chaired and cochaired several IRA and Language Research Association committees. Her many educational awards include being named the Outstanding Teacher Educator and Faculty Member in the School of Teacher Education at SDSU, the Distinguished Research Lecturer from SDSU's Graduate Division of Research, IRA's 1996 Outstanding Teacher Educator of the Year, and the 2011 recipient of the IRA Maryann Manning Outstanding Volunteer Service Award for her continuing work in public schools. Additionally, Diane is a member of both the national and California Reading Halls of Fame. She can be reached at lapp@mail.sdsu.edu.

A ccording to the most recent analysis of ACT scores (ACT, 2011), only 52% of students who took the ACT in 2011 have the reading skills needed to succeed for college work. According to an ACT (2006b) study of skills needed for occupations that do not require a college degree but that provide a living wage, the reading and mathematics skills needed to obtain and hold these jobs are similar to those needed to succeed in college.

To prepare all students to be college and career ready, a set of challenging goals known as the Common Core State Standards has been widely adopted. Although there are three dozen anchor standards, they can be summarized by the goal of having all students be able to read, talk, and write about complex text. ACT (2006a) researchers found that the ability to comprehend complex text provides the best preparation for college:

> *Performance on complex texts is the clearest differentiator in reading between students who are likely to be ready for college and those who are not.* And this is true for both genders, all racial/ethnic groups, and all family income levels. (pp. 16–17, italics in original)

Teachers I have talked to are definitely concerned about the Common Core goal of having students read complex text. There seems to be a misinterpretation that this means simply giving students more difficult text. There is little discussion of the larger question of bolstering instruction so that students can grapple with complex text. Teachers are also concerned about the kinds of texts they will be using. They aren't sure what qualifies as complex text or how to judge the complexity of a text, or, more important, how to develop students' ability to comprehend challenging text. *Text Complexity: Raising Rigor in Reading,* by the distinguished writing team of Douglas Fisher, Nancy Frey, and Diane Lapp, addresses these issues.

A significant portion of the text is devoted to discussing what makes a text complex and how to judge complexity. As the authors point out, if teachers know what makes a text difficult, they can plan lessons to deal with those difficulties.

Developing the ability to read complex text is hard work both for the teacher and the students. Teachers must choose texts that lend themselves to a close reading and need to plan lessons that delve deeply into the text. The authors provide many examples of classroom instruction at the elementary and secondary levels that develops students' ability to engage in a close reading of text and compare information from multiple sources. The authors explain in step-by-step fashion how widely used techniques can be bolstered to develop deeper comprehension. For instance, QAR (Question–Answer Relationships) can be used to plan a series of lessons that gradually draw out a deeper understanding of the text and reinforce the key standard of providing evidence from the text to clarify or justify one's statements about the text.

Developing the ability to read complex text requires a sustained, purposeful effort. As the authors comment in Chapter 1,

> Perhaps one of the mistakes in the past efforts to improve reading achievement has been the removal of struggle. As a profession, we might have made reading tasks too easy. We do not suggest that we should plan students' failure but rather that students should be provided with opportunities to struggle and to learn about themselves as readers when they struggle, persevere, and eventually succeed.

And as they conclude in Chapter 5, "We must commit to our students and help them read increasingly complex texts and read those texts well."

Research-based, thorough, and featuring a rich supply of concrete instructional examples, *Text Complexity* is a must-read for any professional engaged in or contemplating developing the ability to comprehend complex text.

—Thomas G. Gunning
Professor Emeritus, Southern Connecticut State University
Adjunct Professor, Central Connecticut State University

REFERENCES

ACT. (2006a). *Reading between the lines: What the ACT reveals about college readiness in reading.* Iowa City: Author. Available at www.act.org/research/policymakers/pdf/reading_report.pdf

ACT. (2006b). *Ready for college and ready for work: Same or different?* Iowa City: Author. Available at www.act.org/research/policymakers/pdf/ReadinessBrief.pdf

ACT. (2011). *The condition of college & career readiness 2011.* Iowa City: Author. Available at www.act.org/research/policymakers/cccr11/pdf/ConditionofCollegeandCareerReadiness2011.pdf

ACKNOWLEDGMENTS

We would like to thank the reviewers who provided their time and expertise:

- Thomas Gunning, Southern Connecticut State University, Central Connecticut State University
- Shane Templeton, University of Nevada, Reno
- Virginia Goatley, International Reading Association

CHAPTER 1

Text Complexity Is the New Black

There is always something worthy of our attention in reading instruction. It seems that text complexity is now having its day. That's not to say that the previous areas receiving focused attention have been bad or useless. Things are hot for a while, and when they are, new knowledge is generated. At one point, not too long ago, phonics and fluency were hot, but they are less so now (Cassidy & Loveless, 2011). When things are hot, attention is focused, and new insights into readers and the reading process are gained. When things become less hot, it seems that the field has reached some consensus or a new level of understanding for the time being, and therefore attention can be turned to a new area.

Unlike a pendulum, which is often how reading instruction is described, we see this continual research process as a drill, with each subsequent return to a topic resulting in deeper knowledge. In fact, the development of iterative investigations of educational topics was highlighted in a conversation that Diane had with her 80-year-old aunt, a retired teacher. When asked by her aunt what was new in education, Diane replied that she and her colleagues were studying how to support their students in understanding how authors position readers to draw conclusions while reading. Diane's aunt replied, "Well, my heavens, we were teaching that 50 years ago," then paused and added, "But you know, each time some topic in education gets revisited, we learn so much more about how to teach it."

Our renewed attention to text complexity is primarily due to language in the Common Core State Standards. However, like phonics and fluency, this is not the first time that researchers and teachers have paid attention to the materials that students are required to read. We have dipped in and out of the issue of text complexity for years, each time informed by related fields such as linguistics, psychology, and cognition (Graesser, McNamara, & Louwerse, 2011). We used to think about complexity in terms of text difficulty. Now, in revisiting this topic, it's time to go deeper and reconsider text complexity as encompassing both quantitative and qualitative issues as well as the match between readers, texts, and tasks.

Text Complexity Defined

The Common Core State Standards (National Governors Association Center for Best Practices & Council of Chief State School Officers [NGA & CCSSO], 2010b) define text complexity as three interrelated components (see Figure 1.1):

1. *Qualitative dimensions of text complexity:* In the Standards, *qualitative dimensions* and *qualitative factors* refer to those aspects of text complexity best measured or only measurable by an attentive human reader, such as levels of meaning or purpose; structure; language conventionality and clarity; and knowledge demands.

2. *Quantitative dimensions of text complexity:* The terms *quantitative dimensions* and *quantitative factors* refer to those aspects of text complexity, such as word length or frequency, sentence length, and text cohesion, that are difficult if not impossible for a human reader to evaluate efficiently, especially in long texts, and are thus today typically measured by computer software.

Figure 1.1 Dimensions of Text Complexity

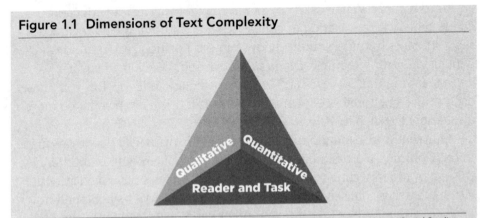

3. *Reader and task considerations:* While the prior two elements of the model focus on the inherent complexity of text, variables specific to particular readers (such as motivation, knowledge, and experiences) and to particular tasks (such as purpose and the complexity of the task assigned and the questions posed) must also be considered when determining whether a text is appropriate for a given student. Such assessments are best made by teachers employing their professional judgment, experience, and knowledge of their students and the subject. (p. 4)

Text complexity is based, in part, on the skills of the reader. When students have the literacy skills necessary to read a text, they are likely to understand what they are reading. It is not hard for students who can decode the words to understand the following passage:

> Annemarie eased the bedroom door open quietly, only a crack, and peeked out. Behind her, Ellen was sitting up, her eyes wide. (Lowry, 1989, p. 43)

Yet, text complexity is more than an analysis of the current skills of readers. Readability, as we explore further in Chapter 2, has a long history and yet still no consensus. *The Literacy Dictionary: The Vocabulary of Reading and Writing* (Harris & Hodges, 1995) defines *readability* as "the ease of comprehension because of style of writing" (p. 203). This definition expands the idea of readability from the skills of the reader to include an analysis of the style of the writing. There are some writing styles that are harder for readers to understand than others. For example, most young adults can follow a plot when told in chronological order but have a much harder time with flashbacks and foreshadowing. In other words, the style of writing may interfere with understanding.

The *Greenwood Dictionary of Education* (Collins & O'Brien, 2003) defines *readability* a bit differently: "The quality and clarity of a piece of written work. Writing that can be understood by those for whom it is written" (p. 295). This definition is interesting, in part, because it requires attention to the intended audience of the text. We can ask ourselves questions about the author's purpose and whether the writing was intended for the audience we have in front of us. Analyzing the intended audience can help readers improve their understanding of a given text. For example, if students understand why the Gettysburg Address was written, they are more likely to comprehend it.

Readability, then, is a balance between the reader's skills and the text itself. How the text acts upon the reader is as important as how the reader acts upon the text. Some texts are more considerate of readers than others. Anderson and Armbruster (1984) identified a number of characteristics of considerate texts, or texts that facilitate comprehension and learning from reading. Their list includes the following:

- *Text structure:* The arrangement system of ideas in the text and the nature of the relationships connecting ideas
- *Coherence:* The extent to which events and concepts are logically and clearly connected and explained
- *Unity:* The extent to which the text retains focus and does not include irrelevant or distracting information
- *Audience appropriateness:* The extent to which the text fits the target readers' probable knowledge base

Readability and considerateness are important aspects of text complexity but are not yet the full picture. It's not as if some pretaught vocabulary, a dab of phonics, and some visualization will help a reader with the assumptions of background knowledge, sophisticated sentence structure, and complex ideas of a text, as in this excerpt:

> Anyway, the fascinating thing was that I read in *National Geographic* that there are more people alive now than have died in all of human history. In other words, if everyone wanted to play Hamlet at once, they couldn't, because there aren't enough skulls! (Foer, 2005, p. 3)

The passage is hard for a number of different reasons. From a quantitative perspective, this text is written at the 10.9 grade level, which is above the average eighth-grade reading level of adults (Kirsch, Jungeblut, Jenkins, & Kolstad, 1993). From a qualitative perspective, there are assumptions about background knowledge hidden in this text. The reference to *National Geographic* signals most readers that the information is verifiable. Understanding the reference to Hamlet and the prop used in the famous soliloquy is critical to making meaning of the second sentence, but a reader could skip that referent and still get the gist of the text.

The deep meaning comes from understanding nuances and inferences. What really makes this text hard is the big idea in the text. The words themselves are not that difficult, but the mathematical computation is mind-boggling and causes most readers to pause and really consider what the author is saying. We ask ourselves, could that really be true? Did I just read that correctly? Is it hyperbole or fact? In doing so, we slowed down, and our fluency rate decreased, but our comprehension soared. In other words, text complexity includes both qualitative and quantitative measures, as well as an analysis of the task required of readers. Reading fiction for pleasure requires a different level of engagement than reading fiction to identify character motives across texts. Reading informational texts to find out about a specific medical condition is different from reading a travel book in preparation for a vacation. The task and purpose of the reading also influence the complexity of the text.

To address this, teachers try to match readers with appropriate texts. Teachers spend countless hours leveling their libraries so students can easily identify appropriate independent reading materials for themselves. Reading widely is a habit that students must develop, but they also need instruction in reading increasingly complex texts so their reading diet is more balanced. We are not suggesting that teachers prevent students from reading widely. Every reader has a diet that includes texts that are easier and harder to read. Nancy regularly reads what she calls the journal of popular culture, more commonly known as *People* magazine, but she also reads research studies, technical information, novels, and news (mainly on her e-book reader). We suggest that more difficult texts with scaffolded instruction should become part of the classroom equation. To ensure that students read complex texts, teachers have to revisit how they match readers with texts and tasks.

Revisiting How We Match Readers and Texts

For decades, teachers have been told that quality instruction requires a careful matching of materials to students. The goal has been to select materials that are neither too difficult nor too easy for the students—a phenomenon sometimes called the Goldilocks rule (Ohlhausen & Jepsen, 1992). Typically, students are assessed on their ability to orally read and comprehend a text. Then, instructional materials are selected to match the students' current performance. The goal has been for students to read texts that they can read with minimal instruction, but there are several problems with this approach. First, basing the match on a student's oral-reading performance is problematic because such an assessment tells little about the student's comprehension. As Kelly (1916) noted almost 100 years ago, "It is generally agreed, I think, that the ability to reproduce is quite a separate ability from the ability to get meaning" (p. 64). Second, text difficulty is reduced over time when students only read things that they can. A fifth grader reading at the fourth-grade level who only reads fourth-grade books will not be prepared for sixth grade. There is evidence that the texts that students read have become easier and less complex in grades 4–12 (Hayes, Wolfer, & Wolfe, 1996). Third, this approach limits what students can read with instruction. As Adams (2010) noted, "More significantly, failing to provide instruction or experience with 'grown-up' text levels seems a risky course toward preparing students for the reading demands of college and life" (p. 5). Finally, there is evidence that students learn, and perhaps even learn more, when they are taught with challenging texts (Morgan, Wilcox, & Eldredge, 2000; O'Connor, Swanson, & Geraghty, 2010).

So, where does the idea of matching readers with texts at their independent reading level come from? The most common formula for selecting these texts consists of three levels (e.g., Betts, 1946). The first, independent level, is considered to be a text that is accurately read at a rate of 95% or higher with a comprehension level of 90–100% as measured by questions. Traditionally, these are the texts that students are asked to read on their own, at home or at school. Students who read a text with 89% or less accuracy and less than 75% comprehension are considered to be at their frustration level because the number of errors interferes too greatly with meaning. In most cases, teachers avoid assigning students frustration-level texts. Text read accurately at a rate of 90–94% and a comprehension rate of 75–89% is called instructional level. Teachers use instructional-level texts because they provide students with enough challenges to focus their attention on their problem-solving skills without being so difficult that all meaning is lost. However, these percentages have been challenged. For example, Powell (1970) recommends 85% as a better predictor of student learning, which would result in students reading harder texts. However, the 95% rate persists in most classrooms despite the lack of evidence that it is effective.

Although it has become a commonly accepted practice to strictly adhere to these levels when matching students to texts for reading instruction, concerns about this reader–text match have proliferated in educational literature for decades (Chall & Conard, 1991; Killgallon, 1942; O'Connor, Bell, et al., 2002; Weber, 1968). Teachers know that when students are asked to read complex texts by themselves, they struggle and often do not succeed because they do not have the appropriate bank of related language, knowledge, skills, or metacognition to be able to comprehend the information. Teachers also realize that when they provide the needed instructional supports, students have greater success with reading materials that could be initially identified as being at their frustrational levels. The text difficulty level is not the real issue. Instruction is. Teachers can scaffold and support students, which will determine the amount of their learning and literacy independence.

Text Complexity and the Common Core State Standards

The Common Core State Standards challenge teachers to provide scaffolded instructional supports for every learner and to do so with complex and difficult texts. When first hearing this, teachers may be concerned because they have always attempted to assess how well each student reads a text to determine appropriate instructional levels, believing that without a text level/student level placement match, a student will have little success. As realized from a careful reading of the history of educational assessment (Johnston, 1984), there is little research supporting this text placement practice, and what research there is seems to be unrealistic because it promotes the narrow idea that students can only read materials at their instructional placement level. As Bruner (1964), Vygotsky (1962), and every classroom teacher knows, with appropriately scaffolded instruction that is indeed based on continuous teacher assessment of the increasing bank of knowledge and language that a student has on a topic being studied, a student can learn to read texts that are beyond his or her instructional level and hopefully learn how to support his or her own reading of difficult text when the teacher is no longer at the reader's side. As Shanahan (2011) noted,

If the teacher is doing little to support the students' transactions with text then I suspect more learning will accrue with somewhat easier texts. However, if reasonable levels of instructional support are available then students are likely to thrive when working with harder texts. (para. 11)

Selecting appropriate reading materials for students is hard, especially when students should be reading each day in every content area. Grade-level expectations drive some of the selections, but wise teachers also know that students cannot independently learn from texts that they can't read. In fact, there is no evidence that simply assigning fifth-grade reading materials to a student who reads at the second-grade level will help the student grow as a skilled, independent, or motivated reader. Yet, limiting that student to second-grade materials constricts the learning and fails to ensure that the student develops new habits and skills in reading. Making the appropriate match is a dilemma that is gaining a great deal of attention (Gewertz, 2011). The idea is not to either limit a student to a low-level text or allow him or her to struggle without support in a difficult text, but instead to provide texts and couple them with instruction. As students progress, they should be given increasingly challenging materials and taught, encouraged, and supported to use deeper skills of analysis.

With the introduction of the Common Core State Standards in 2010, the spotlight on text complexity renewed attention on reading materials. More than a text gradient, the developers of the Common Core State Standards invite us to foreground the texts themselves as an essential element in reading instruction. Although materials have been important, they have not always been viewed as a way to advance readers. Instead, the focus has been on matching students to the reading. The thinking has been, "If I know the reader thoroughly enough, I can find the reading." Although this is correct, it is insufficient. By adding complex texts to the formula, we recognize that the reading itself can be a scaffold to knowledge and also to one's reading prowess.

The Common Core State Standards for English Language Arts are organized around 10 anchor standards that extend from kindergarten through 12th grade. Anchor standard 10 in the College and Career Readiness Anchor Standards for Reading section for all grade levels, which is the focus of this book, covers text complexity. This standard's wording is deceptively simple: "Read and comprehend complex literary and informational texts independently and proficiently" (NGA & CCSSO,

2010a, p. 10). This anchor standard calls for students to be able to read independently, and the text exemplars cited in Appendix B of the standards are hard. However, these should not be misconstrued as a reading list, with teachers simply ordering lots of hard books and then standing by to watch students be defeated by them. It would set the field back decades if in response to these standards, teachers assigned students hours of independent reading that was devoid of instruction. We cannot help but recall our own experiences in searching used book stores for yellow and black paperbacks that held the answers to the questions that our teachers might ask us about the hard texts that we were assigned but did not read. Table 1.1 is a small sample of the kinds of complex texts identified as exemplars in the Common Core State Standards.

A close reading of the standards reveals a clear call for teacher support in teaching students to read complex texts. Under the heading "A focus on results rather than means," the document goes on to say,

> By emphasizing required achievements, the Standards leave room for teachers, curriculum developers, and states to determine how those goals should be reached and what additional topics should be addressed. Thus, the

Table 1.1 Sample of Complex Texts at Various Grade Levels

Grades	Narrative Text Example	Informational Text Example
K and 1	*Green Eggs and Ham* by Dr. Seuss	*My Five Senses* by Aliki
2 and 3	*The Raft* by Jim LaMarche	*Where Do Polar Bears Live?* by Sarah L. Thomson
4 and 5	*Bud, Not Buddy* by Christopher Paul Curtis	*Toys! Amazing Stories Behind Some Great Inventions* by Don Wulffson
6–8	*A Wrinkle in Time* by Madeleine L'Engle	*Narrative of the Life of Frederick Douglass, an American Slave, Written by Himself* by Frederick Douglass
9 and 10	*Fahrenheit 451* by Ray Bradbury	"Hope, Despair and Memory" by Elie Wiesel
11+	*Their Eyes Were Watching God* by Zora Neale Hurston	"Mother Tongue" by Amy Tan

Note. List extracted from *Common Core State Standards for English Language Arts and Literacy in History/ Social Studies, Science, and Technical Subjects: Appendix B: Text Exemplars and Sample Performance Tasks* (pp. 4–12), by National Governors Association Center for Best Practices & Council of Chief State School Officers, 2010, Washington, DC: Authors. Copyright 2010 by the National Governors Association Center for Best Practices and the Council of Chief State School Officers. All rights reserved.

Standards do not mandate such things as a particular writing process or the full range of metacognitive strategies that students may need to monitor and direct their thinking and learning. *Teachers are thus free to provide students with whatever tools and knowledge their professional judgment and experience identify as most helpful for meeting the goals set out in the Standards* [italics added]. (NGA & CCSSO, 2010a, p. 4)

In other words, the Common Core State Standards acknowledge that teachers have to figure out how to help their students access complex texts and that teachers should use their professional judgments to accomplish this task. In the past, teachers were held captive to the script (R.J. Meyer, 2002) and were required to read verbatim from a teacher's manual. Teachers felt like zombies going through the motions of teaching (Demko, 2010), but the standards change that and place the responsibility on the teacher. What is not negotiable is student achievement; what is negotiable is how teachers get their students to read worthy and complex texts. Teaching students to read grade-level and more complex texts requires first and foremost an understanding of what makes a text complex.

The Case for Struggle

When reading gets hard, readers slow down and consciously use strategies to try to make sense of the text. That's what happened when we read the passage that included referents to *National Geographic* and Hamlet. It's not that the reader slows down so much that he or she gets lost but that the reader slows down enough to become strategic. Yet, being strategic is not the goal of reading. Deep comprehension is the primary goal. Reading requires automaticity—the systematic and automatic deployment of cognitive behaviors to make meaning of the text. When readers deploy cognitive strategies automatically, they are considered skilled readers. As Afflerbach, Pearson, and Paris (2008) point out, "reading skills operate without the reader's deliberate control or conscious awareness … [t]his has important, positive consequences for each reader's limited working memory" (p. 368). Strategies, on the contrary, are "effortful and deliberate" and occur during initial learning, when the text is more difficult for the reader to understand (p. 369). Table 1.2 summarizes the differences between skills and strategies. Strategies become skills with instruction and practice. The challenge is to apply these skills to increasingly complex and

Table 1.2 Comparing Skills and Strategies

Strategy	Skills
A conscious plan under the control of the reader.	An automatic procedure that readers use unconsciously.
Requires thought about which plan to use and when to use them.	Do not require thought, interpretation, or choice.
Are process-oriented, cognitive procedures the reader uses, generally unobservable in nature.	Are observable behaviors, found on taxonomies, skills tests, or answers to questions.
Instruction focuses on the reasoning process readers use as they interact with text.	Instruction focuses on repeated use until it becomes habitual.

Note. From *Good Habits, Great Readers: Building the Literacy Community* (p. 9), by N. Frey, D. Fisher, and A. Berkin, 2009, Boston: Allyn & Bacon. Copyright 2009 by Pearson. Reprinted with permission.

diverse texts. In doing so, readers will generalize their skills and become proficient readers who can read widely. This requires readers to struggle a bit as they apply their skills in new situations.

Perhaps one of the mistakes in the past efforts to improve reading achievement has been the removal of struggle. As a profession, we may have made reading tasks too easy. We do not suggest that we should plan students' failure but rather that students should be provided with opportunities to struggle and to learn about themselves as readers when they struggle, persevere, and eventually succeed.

This concept of supportive struggle is known as productive failure (Kapur, 2008). Productive failure provides students an opportunity to struggle with something and learn from the mistakes they make along the way. Again, it's not planned failure but rather an opportunity to struggle with something and learn along the way. Consider the worthy struggle for a group of sixth-grade students reading the following from *Faithful Elephants: A True Story of Animals, People, and War* by Yukio Tsuchiya (1951/1988), which recounts the bombing of Tokyo in the final months of World War II:

> "What would happen if bombs hit the zoo? If the cages were broken and dangerous animals escaped to run wild through the city, it would be terrible! Therefore, by command of the Army, all of the lions, tigers, leopards, bears, and big snakes were poisoned to death." (p. 9)

Again, the individual words are not that hard (seventh-grade level), but the ideas are complex and tragic. Given that the text is a picture book, some teachers and students initially believe that it is too easy. However, the content is tough, and the ideas are complex. More than one adult has burst into tears while reading this book.

As students talked about what the character in the book says and considered the time at which this was written, they struggled to figure out why the animals were killed. The students struggled with the moral and ethical dilemmas that the text poses. Using evidence from the text to justify his response, Justin said, "This is a memory from the guy at the memorial. He's remembering this. I think so because of how sad he was at the end and how he was taking care of the marker at the beginning." Marla, also using evidence from the text, responded, "I agree with you. The title says that it's true, and I think that this was a time when they were worried about war and tried to protect people." The students' conversation continued, and they struggled to understand a text written at a different time for a different audience. Yet, through that struggle, they came to an understanding. As one member of the group said, "Sometimes wars are necessary, but there are always bystanders hurt along the way. I never thought about the animals, but I guess that they are innocent bystanders of human wars, too."

All readers should be given opportunities to analyze complex texts. In a first-grade classroom, students read *The Sun* by Justin McCory Martin (2007) to become familiar with the Sun's structure and role in our solar system. However, this is only the first step in deeply comprehending concepts about the Sun. Mr. Connolly realizes that students must next be exposed to other source materials on the same topic so they can compare and contrast information and texts as they build their knowledge, language, and text investigation skills. With additional articles, books, websites, and photographs about the Sun, he and his students can take a close look at several topically similar informational texts and make comparisons about the texts.

Mr. Connolly is addressing the grade 1 reading standard for informational text: "Identify basic similarities in and differences between the two texts on the same topic (e.g., in illustrations, descriptions, or procedures)" (NGA & CCSSO, 2010a, p. 13). For students to master this expectation, he realizes that they must be taught to attend to details in the text to make a contrastive analysis. Even young students can be taught to take notes about what they are learning. A chart such as Figure 1.2 enables students to compile information for a closer understanding of a topic as understood through analysis of several texts.

By analyzing these texts with their teacher, Mr. Connolly, the students were able to understand the topical knowledge and language because he provided instruction that involved modeling, guiding, and observing recursively through continual assessment of the students' performance as related to the lesson purpose. He considers the task, as well as the readers and the text, to develop sound instruction. As this example briefly illustrates, to fully comprehend and analyze texts, students need their teacher to guide their reading and discussion as they scrutinize these texts.

This level of analysis applies to both narrative and informational texts. The Langston Hughes (1958/1996) short story "Thank You, M'am," often

Figure 1.2 Learning About a Topic

Text 1: Important Ideas	Text 2: Important Ideas	Text 3: Important Ideas
• • •	• • •	• • •
What I Learned From Text 1	**What I Learned From Text 2**	**What I Learned From Text 3**
• • •	• • •	• • •
What I Learned From Reading the Texts		
• • •		

included in anthologies, can be revisited for a deeper level of analysis of character development. Ms. Chin and her fifth-grade students returned to a text several times to accomplish the lesson purpose. In the following discussion, notice how she scaffolded the instruction to ensure that they gained the identified insights.

Ms. Chin began this lesson sequence by telling students that the purpose was to discover how characters' lives could be changed by chance encounters or fate. She shared that while reading, the students would investigate how the author shows them that the characters' lives can change from the beginning of a story to the end. She told the students that the author offers clues to help them identify the development of characters and that by closely investigating those text clues and language, they would be able to see the changes unfolding in the characters' development.

Next, Ms. Chin asked the students to independently read the text so they could familiarize themselves with the characters, the story, the language, and how the characters change over the course of the story. She invited the students to annotate the text and create notes by paying attention to the words, phrases, and dialogue that the author used to help readers understand the development of the characters.

After the initial reading, she asked the students to talk with their partners about the story, describe the characters by using evidence from the text, and note how the characters changed from the beginning of the story to the end. When she heard a student say, "The woman is large. It says so right here. And she is mean because it says that she kicked him right square in the blue jean sitter," Ms. Chin knew that the students must be supported in reading more deeply to understand why the character acted as she had.

Initiating a second reading, Ms. Chin reminded the students that authors often write stories about characters who transform, or change, from the beginning of the text to the end. She explained that she was going to think aloud while reading, with the intent of finding out more about the characters. She asked them to follow along as she read:

"'The large woman simply turned around and kicked him right square in his blue-jeaned sitter. Then she reached down, picked the boy up by his shirtfront, and shook him until his teeth rattled.' While reading, I was picturing a big woman but not a weak woman. I know this because she is able to kick this boy and pick him up by his shirt. This sounds like a strong woman. I bet the boy wished he hadn't messed with her. He sounds scared since his teeth rattled.

"The woman asked the boy if she was bothering him, and the boy said no. It also says that 'you put yourself in contact with me...[and] if you think that that contact is not going to last awhile, you got another thought coming.' This tells me that their encounter, their meeting, will have a big impact on this boy's life. Perhaps he will be changed forever. I wonder if there are more clues about how this boy's life is changing.

"Yes, I know he is changing because it says that after he looked at her, 'there was a long pause. A very long pause. After he had dried his face and not knowing what else to do, dried it again, the boy turned around, wondering what next.' Later, it says, 'The boy's mouth opened. Then he frowned, not knowing he frowned.' I think he is very touched that this woman is helping him, and maybe nobody has ever helped him before, so he doesn't know what to do or say.

"Here at the end, it says that 'the boy wanted to say something other than, 'Thank you, m'am,'...but although his lips moved, he couldn't even say that." I'm imagining his lips opening, but the words of gratitude couldn't come out. I really think no one had treated the boy like this, and he was used to being mistreated or neglected, so I think his life had been changed by this woman's kindness."

After thinking aloud, Ms. Chin and the students engaged in a discussion using a series of text-dependent questions to help them uncover more evidence regarding the main character's transformation. The following are some of the questions discussed:

- How does the woman feel about the boy? Is she angry at him? Does she like him? How do you know?

- At what point in the story does the woman show that she cares for the boy? How do you know?

- Describe the boy. What does his physical appearance and behavior tell you?

- What examples can you find that show that the woman understands the boy very well?

- How do you think Roger's encounter with the woman altered his life?

After the discussion, Ms. Chin asked the students to write about the characters. Now that her students understood how the characters had changed, she asked how a second encounter might go. She asked them to write, assuming that the characters would meet again. The students each wrote a dialogue between the boy and the woman, describing their second encounter—a week, a month, or a year later.

By analyzing these dialogues, Ms. Chin was able to assess whether her students had gained an understanding of the developing characters and also an understanding that characters change over time as a result of their experiences. Based on this information, she was able to plan subsequent instruction. As this example illustrates, to fully comprehend and analyze a text, and regardless of their instructional reading levels, students can read, discuss, and scrutinize a text multiple times to conduct a deep analysis and comprehension, with their teacher acting as a guide. Each revisit strengthens the readers' base of knowledge, language, concrete reasoning, evaluative judgment, and text analysis skills.

Conclusion

It's difficult to create a simple lesson to teach students to understand a complex text. It takes time to develop the thinking skills necessary to read complex texts. It also takes really good instruction. We think it is possible to teach students to read complex texts, but that teaching requires more than assigning students hard books and hoping that they get better at reading. Teaching starts with a deep understanding about what makes text complex. In the chapters that follow, we explore quantitative and qualitative factors of text complexity, as well as tasks that increase or decrease that complexity. We also focus on instruction and assessment of complex texts through close readings and extensive discussions. With this understanding, lessons can be developed that ensure that students are prepared for the wide range of reading and writing that they will do throughout their lives.

As we discuss and illustrate with examples shared throughout this book, close reading requires a revisiting of how texts are both read and taught. With appropriate instructional supports, texts can be reread and analyzed to unearth complex structures, themes, and insights. Revisiting a text offers the possibility that all readers will be challenged to think more deeply about texts that they are already able to comfortably and fluently decode and understand at a surface level. The emphasis can then be on close reading even after automaticity has been achieved. This analysis can be related to the specific content, such as events, chronology, motives, time sequence (Warren, Nicholas, & Trabasso, 1977), propositional hierarchies (Kintsch, 1974), story grammar (Rumelhart, 1975), and logical structures (B.J.F. Meyer, 1975).

As discussed in subsequent chapters, determining a reader's success during close reading involves an analysis of many factors. By considering a three-part model of (1) quantitative measures of the text; (2) qualitative considerations about content, structure, and cohesion; and (3) the reader and the tasks, teachers can make instructional decisions from a broader base. It is essential to revisit the reader–text match to maximize instruction with complex texts so learning can occur for every student all day long. As a reviewer of this book wrote, *"readability* is not the same as *learnability."*

REFERENCES

Adams, M.J. (2010). Advancing our students' language and literacy: The challenge of complex texts. *American Educator, 34*(4), 3–11, 53.

Afflerbach, P., Pearson, P.D., & Paris, S.G. (2008). Clarifying differences between reading skills and reading strategies. *The Reading Teacher, 61*(5), 364–373. doi:10.1598/RT.61.5.1

Anderson, T.H., & Armbruster, B.B. (1984). Content area textbooks. In R.C. Anderson, J. Osborn, & R.J. Tierney (Eds.), *Learning to read in American schools: Basal readers and content texts* (pp. 193–226). Hillsdale, NJ: Erlbaum.

Betts, E.A. (1946). *Foundations of reading instruction.* New York: American Book.

Bruner, J.S. (1964). The course of cognitive development. *American Psychologist, 19,* 1–15.

Cassidy, J., & Loveless, D.J. (2011, October/November). Taking our pulse in a time of uncertainty: Results of the 2012 *What's Hot, What's Not* literacy survey. *Reading Today,* 16–21.

Chall, J.S., & Conard, S.S. (with Harris-Sharples, S.). (1991). *Should textbooks challenge students? The case for easier or harder books.* New York: Teachers College Press.

Collins, J.W., III, & O'Brien, N.P. (Eds.). (2003). *The Greenwood dictionary of education.* Westport, CT: Greenwood.

Demko, M. (with Hedrick, W.). (2010). Teachers become zombies: The ugly side of scripted reading curriculum. *Voices From the Middle, 17*(3), 62–64.

Frey, N., Fisher, D., & Berkin, A. (2009). *Good habits, great readers: Building the literacy community.* Boston: Allyn & Bacon.

Gewertz, C. (2011). Teachers seek ways to gauge rigor of texts. *Education Week, 30*(24), 1, 12–13.

Graesser, A.C., McNamara, D.S., & Louwerse, M.M. (2011). Methods of automated text analysis. In M.L. Kamil, P.D. Pearson, E.B. Moje, & P.P. Afflerbach (Eds.), *Handbook of reading research* (Vol. IV, pp. 34–53). New York: Routledge.

Harris, T.L., & Hodges, R.E. (Eds.). (1995). *The literacy dictionary: The vocabulary of reading and writing.* Newark, DE: International Reading Association.

Hayes, D.P., Wolfer, L.T., & Wolfe, M.F. (1996). Schoolbook simplification and its relation to the decline in SAT-Verbal scores. *American Educational Research Journal, 33*(2), 489–508.

Johnston, P. (1984). Assessment in reading. In P.D. Pearson, R. Barr, M.L. Kamil, & P. Mosenthal (Eds.), *Handbook of reading research* (pp. 147–182). New York: Longman.

Kapur, M. (2008). Productive failure. *Cognition and Instruction, 26*(3), 379–424. doi:10.1080/07370000802212669

Kelly, F.J. (1916). The Kansas Silent Reading Tests. *Journal of Educational Psychology, 7*(2), 63–80. doi:10.1037/h0073542

Killgallon, P.A. (1942). *A study of relationships among certain pupil adjustments in language situations.* Unpublished doctoral dissertation, Pennsylvania State College, University Park.

Kintsch, W.E. (with Crothers, E.J. et al.). (1974). *The representation of meaning in memory.* Hillsdale, NJ: Erlbaum.

Kirsch, I.S., Jungeblut, A., Jenkins, L., & Kolstad, A. (1993). *Adult literacy in America: A first look at the findings of the National Adult Literacy Survey* (NCES 1993-275). Washington, DC: National Center for Education Statistics, Office of Educational Research and Improvement, U.S. Department of Education.

Meyer, B.J.F. (1975). *The organization of prose and its effect on memory.* Amsterdam: North-Holland.

Meyer, R.J. (2002). Captives of the script: Killing us softly with phonics. *Language Arts, 79*(6), 452–461.

Morgan, A., Wilcox, B.R., & Eldredge, J.L. (2000). Effect of difficulty levels on second-grade delayed readers using dyad reading. *The Journal of Educational Research, 94*(2), 113–119. doi:10.1080/00220670009598749

National Governors Association Center for Best Practices & Council of Chief State School Officers. (2010a). *Common Core State Standards for English language arts and literacy in history/social studies, science, and technical subjects.* Washington, DC: Authors. Retrieved January 7, 2012, from www.corestandards.org/assets/CCSSI_ELA%20Standards.pdf

National Governors Association Center for Best Practices & Council of Chief State School Officers. (2010b). *Common Core State Standards for English language arts and literacy in history/social studies, science, and technical subjects: Appendix A: Research supporting key elements of the standards and glossary of key terms.* Washington, DC: Authors. Retrieved January 7, 2012, from www.corestandards.org/assets/Appendix_A.pdf

National Governors Association Center for Best Practices & Council of Chief State School Officers. (2010c). *Common Core State Standards for English language arts and literacy in history/social studies, science, and technical subjects: Appendix B: Text exemplars and sample performance tasks.* Washington, DC: Authors. Retrieved January 7, 2012, from www.corestandards.org/assets/Appendix_B.pdf

O'Connor, R.E., Bell, K.M., Harty, K.R., Larkin, L.K., Sackor, S.M., & Zigmond, N. (2002). Teaching reading to poor readers in the intermediate grades: A comparison of text difficulty. *Journal of Educational Psychology, 94*(3), 474–485. doi:10.1037/0022-0663.94.3.474

O'Connor, R.E., Swanson, H.L., & Geraghty, C. (2010). Improvement in reading rate under independent and difficult text levels: Influences on word and comprehension skills. *Journal of Educational Psychology, 102*(1), 1–19. doi:10.1037/a0017488

Ohlhausen, M.M., & Jepsen, M. (1992). Lessons from Goldilocks: "Somebody's been choosing my books but I can make my own choices now!" *The New Advocate, 5*(1), 31–46.

Powell, W.R. (1970). Reappraising the criteria for interpreting informal reading inventories. In D.L. DeBoer (Ed.), *Reading diagnosis and evaluation* (pp. 100–109). Newark, DE: International Reading Association.

Rumelhart, D.E. (1975). Notes on a schema for stories. In D.G. Bobrow & A. Collins (Eds.), *Representation and understanding: Studies in cognitive science* (pp. 211–236). New York: Academic.

Shanahan, T. (2011, August 21). Rejecting instructional level theory [Web log post]. Retrieved January 7, 2012, from www.shanahanonliteracy.com/search/label/text%20difficulty

Vygotsky, L.S. (1962). *Thought and language* (E. Hanfmann & G. Vakar, Eds. & Trans.). Cambridge, MA: MIT Press.

Warren, W.H., Nicholas, D.W., & Trabasso, T. (1977). Event chains and inferences in understanding narratives. In R.O. Freedle (Ed.), Advances in discourse processes: Vol. 1. Discourse production and comprehension (pp. 5–27). Norwood, NJ: Ablex.

Weber, R. (1968). The study of oral reading errors: A survey of the literature. *Reading Research Quarterly, 4*(1), 96–119.

LITERATURE CITED

Foer, J.S. (2005). *Extremely loud and incredibly close.* Boston: Houghton Mifflin.

Hughes, L. (1996). "Thank you, ma'm." In A.S. Harper (Ed.), *The short stories of Langston Hughes* (pp. 223–226). New York: Hill and Wang. (Original work published 1958)

Martin, J.M. (2007). *The sun.* New York: Scholastic.

Lowry, L. (1989). *Number the stars.* New York: Bantam Doubleday Dell.

Tsuchiya, Y. (1988). *Faithful elephants: A true story of animals, people, and war* (T.T. Dykes, Trans.). Boston: Houghton Mifflin. (Original work published 1951)

CHAPTER 2

Quantitative Measures of Text Complexity

The terms quantitative dimensions *and* quantitative factors *refer to those aspects of text complexity, such as word length or frequency, sentence length, and text cohesion, that are difficult if not impossible for a human reader to evaluate efficiently, especially in long texts, and are thus today typically measured by computer software.*

—NGA & CCSSO, 2010, p. 4

One way to think about text complexity is through quantitative measures. These primarily focus on the characteristics of the words themselves and their appearance in sentences and paragraphs. Conventional quantitative text measures do not take into account the functions of words and phrases to convey meaning but rather focus on those elements that lend themselves to being counted, and therefore calculated. These surface structures are collectively described as readability formulas and primarily measure semantic difficulty and sentence complexity. Gunning (2003) reports that although more than 100 readability formulas have been developed since the 1920s, only a handful are regularly used today.

To provide a historical context for thinking about the components of readability formulas, we need to review some of the history of reading research. As we noted in Chapter 1, text complexity has a long history and has, at times, been in vogue, although at other times, it has been on the back burner. In 1935, Gray and Leary analyzed 228 variables that affected reading difficulty and divided them into four types: content, style, format, and organization. The researchers could not find an easy way to measure content, format, or organization, but they could measure variables of style. From their list of 17 variables of style, they selected five to create a formula:

1. Average sentence length

2. Number of different hard words

3. Number of personal pronouns

4. Percentage of unique words

5. Number of prepositional phrases

The formula had a correlation of 0.645 with comprehension, as measured by reading tests given to 800 adults. These criteria have been applied to varying degrees in nearly all readability formulas since Gray and Leary's original studies. In other words, quantitative measures to predict text difficulty have been around for a long time. The Common Core State Standards have refocused attention on these issues that have been studied for decades. Educators today are well served in understanding where these formulas come from and how they were developed.

Before delving further into quantitative measures, it is important that we compare and contrast these with qualitative measures (see Chapter 3). There is some overlap in what each examines. To varying degrees, each identifies the characteristics of a text that can pose a challenge to a reader: the semantic and syntactic structures, vocabulary load, organization, and linguistic features such as parts of speech and cohesion among sentences. The primary variable is not what is analyzed but rather how it is analyzed. Each methodology measures some things exceedingly well, and yet each is inadequate for measuring other aspects of text difficulty. Quantitative measures rely on computers, whereas qualitative measures rely on humans. To fully understand a text and its complexity, both are needed.

Ultimately, it is the reader who decides the difficulty of a text. Difficulty, like beauty, is in the eye of the beholder. As you read this chapter, keep in mind that readability formulas predict the level of difficulty of a text, but the only way to truly determine difficulty is to ask the reader to read. In Chapter 4, we examine this reader–text interaction by considering how the reader and the assigned task affect the text difficulty. To overlook the qualitative dimensions of a text, or the transaction that occurs between the reader and the text, would allow for a serious miscalculation. It's analogous to looking at the Grand Canyon from only one viewpoint. You can see a slice, maybe even a meaningful portion, but you can't truly appreciate its dimensions until you have seen it from above, below, and at various points in between.

Word-Level Analysis

There is a strong foundation for using quantitative measures to determine the relative level of challenge posed to a reader. The first level of analysis is at the word level. The overall length of the word suggests the degree to which a reader must decode the word, with single-syllable words considered to be easier than multisyllabic ones. Also, the frequency with which the word appears in a language supposes its familiarity to the reader. The Brown corpus, developed in 1967 by Kucera and Francis at Brown University, used computational analysis of over a million words drawn from 500 written sources, including novels, newspapers, and scientific journals, to determine each word's degree of occurrence in American English. The researchers determined that the words *the, to,* and *of* collectively comprised 13% of the corpus, or body of words in the language (Wikipedia, 2011). Word frequency lists used in readability formulas may number in the thousands or even millions, but they all attempt to rank order a word's frequency of use within specific text types. The most comprehensive review of word frequency completed to date is *The Educator's Word Frequency Guide* (Zeno, Ivens, Millard, & Duvvuri, 1995), which is a listing of the printed words that has been organized by how often a particular word appears in texts encountered by students at a specific grade level. The listing is also available in a searchable software version through Questar Assessment (www.questarai.com). In addition, this resource can calculate the Advantage–TASA Open Standard (ATOS) readability formula used with Accelerated Reader software. One can also use the online WordCount program (www.wordcount.org/main.php), which presents the 86,800 most frequently used English words, ranked in order of frequency.

However, word frequency alone is an incomplete measure of difficulty because the context in which the word appears can increase its difficulty. To focus more specifically on school-age readers, in the 1940s, Dale, later aided by O'Rourke, began developing a list of words that 80% of fourth graders would recognize and know. Over time, these evolved into a list of 3,000 words (Chall & Dale, 1995). The genius of this work is that the researchers didn't just make a list; they also applied it as a way of determining the difficulty that readers might experience depending on the number of words not on the list. In other words (excuse the pun), a text with a higher percentage of words not among the 3,000 could indicate a degree of difficulty. Thus, a text with the words *field, meadow,* or *pasture,* which appear on the list, would not be deemed as difficult as a text that uses the words *steppe* or *mead,* which do not appear on the list. The application of such a word list takes into account what the reader might be expected to know as well as the vocabulary demand of a word. Other word frequency lists developed since then build a corpus, or body, that is reflective of the use of a group of people, such as fourth graders or students entering high school. A key factor in this list is that Dale and O'Rourke (1976) tested and retested these words with students over a period of several decades and eventually published the list as *The Living Word Vocabulary, the Words We Know: A National Vocabulary Inventory.* This sets it apart from other frequency lists.

Sentence-Level Analysis

A second level of analysis included in nearly all quantitative readability formulas is the length of the sentence. The number of words in a sentence is a proxy for several syntactic and semantic demands on a reader, such as prepositional phrases, dependent clauses, adjectives, and adverbs. Taken together, these press a reader's working memory to keep a multitude of concepts and connections in mind (Kintsch, 1974). Consider the following sentence from Sandra Cisneros's short story "Eleven," about a young girl embarrassed by the shabbiness of her sweater:

> This is when I wish I wasn't eleven, because all the years inside of me—ten, nine, eight, seven, six, five, four, three, two, and one—are pushing at the back of my eyes when I put one arm through one sleeve of the sweater that smells like cottage cheese, and then the other arm through the other and stand there with my arms apart like if the sweater hurts me and it does, all itchy and full of germs that aren't even mine. (1991, p. 8)

At 84 words, this sentence requires the reader to process several concepts simultaneously: the sweater and its smell and feel, the clause that lists a descending sequence of numbers, and the use of the word *other* to refer first to her arm and then to the sleeve. An analysis of individual words alone would be insufficient; all but two (*itchy* and *germs*) appear on the Dale–Chall word list. We deliberately selected a long sentence to illustrate the point that sentence length can be a valid indicator of the cognitive load—except when it's not.

Very short text can also tax a reader:

For sale: Baby shoes, never worn.

Legend has it that this six-word story was written by Ernest Hemingway to settle a bar bet (neither the bar bet story or the six-word one have ever been confirmed). These six words score as a second-grade text (2.4 using the Flesch–Kincaid readability formula), and all of the words appear on the Dale–Chall word list. However, the level of inference and background knowledge needed to understand this text would challenge young readers. Readability formulas offer us a level of quantitative analysis that is not readily apparent but should be augmented by the qualitative analyses that only a human reader can offer (Anderson, Hiebert, Scott, & Wilkinson, 1985).

We have discussed issues of word length, syllables, frequency of occurrence, and word lists because they are widely regarded as proxies for the time needed for a reader to read the text and the extent to which it taxes a reader's working memory (Just & Carpenter, 1992). As noted by Gunning (2003), these variables can be used as measures of semantic complexity. His insights echo many of the dimensions described by Gray and Leary in 1935:

- Number of words not on a list of words tested and found to be known by most students at a certain grade level
- Number of words not on a list of high-frequency words
- Grade levels of the words
- Number of syllables in the words
- Number of letters in a word
- Number of different words in a selection
- Number of words having three or more syllables
- Frequency with which the words appear in print (p. 176)

Conventional Readability Formulas

Conventional readability formulas have been used extensively as a means to replace outdated grade-level formulas for rating text difficulty. An advantage of these formulas is that teachers can easily compute them

Figure 2.1 Excerpt From *The Hunger Games*

After the anthem, the tributes file back into the Training Center lobby and onto the elevators. I make sure to veer into a car that does not contain Peeta. The crowd slows our entourages of stylists and mentors and chaperones, so we have only each other for company. No one speaks. My elevator stops to deposit four tributes before I am alone and then find the doors opening on the twelfth floor. Peeta has only just stepped from his car when I slam my palms into his chest. He loses his balance and crashes into an ugly urn filled with fake flowers.

Note. From *The Hunger Games* (p. 134), by Suzanne Collins, New York: Scholastic. Copyright 2008 by Suzanne Collins.

using any reading material. A few of the more common formulas and how they are used to determine readability are reviewed next. As a way to highlight some of the differences among these, we analyze a passage from *The Hunger Games* by Suzanne Collins (2008). This passage (see Figure 2.1) contains a proper noun (*Peeta*, a character's name) and some words that have been introduced previously, such as *tributes*. According to Scholastic, overall readability of the book is 5.3 grade level, but the publisher recommends the content for students in grades 7 and 8 (it should be noted that all of us love this book despite graduating from middle school decades ago). Individual passages within the book are harder, as we will see, which means other passages must be easier. This is an important point in considering quantitative difficulty—the law of averages is at work. That does not mean that the entire text is readable just because the average suggests it is so. Having said that, readability formulas can be used to guide text selection in a quick and easy way. They just aren't the only guide available to teachers.

Fry

The primary appeal of this formula is its ease of use—and that it does not require any specialized software or hardware. Fry (2002) designed this simple readability rating so it can be calculated using the graph in Figure 2.2. The teacher selects three 100-word passages from the book, preferably one each from the beginning, middle, and end. Next, the teacher counts the number of sentences and syllables in each passage, then averages each of the two factors (i.e., number of syllables, number of sentences). These

Figure 2.2 Fry Readability Graph

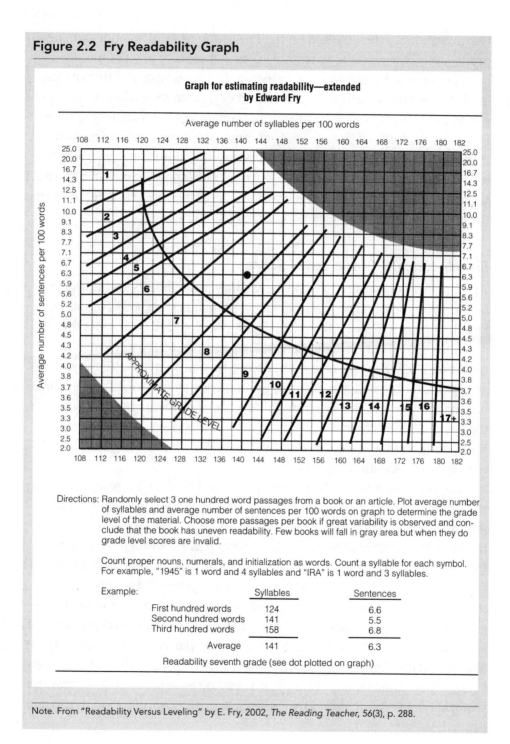

Graph for estimating readability—extended
by Edward Fry

Average number of syllables per 100 words

Directions: Randomly select 3 one hundred word passages from a book or an article. Plot average number of syllables and average number of sentences per 100 words on graph to determine the grade level of the material. Choose more passages per book if great variability is observed and conclude that the book has uneven readability. Few books will fall in gray area but when they do grade level scores are invalid.

Count proper nouns, numerals, and initialization as words. Count a syllable for each symbol. For example, "1945" is 1 word and 4 syllables and "IRA" is 1 word and 3 syllables.

Example:	Syllables	Sentences
First hundred words	124	6.6
Second hundred words	141	5.5
Third hundred words	158	6.8
Average	141	6.3

Readability seventh grade (see dot plotted on graph)

Note. From "Readability Versus Leveling" by E. Fry, 2002, *The Reading Teacher, 56*(3), p. 288.

two averages are then plotted on the Fry graph to yield an approximate grade level. This readability formula does not require any computer calculations, as the algorithm is embedded in the graph. For this reason, the Fry readability formula is popular among teachers who need a quick method for gaining a sense of the approximate level of difficulty of a text. However, the formula does not rely on any specific vocabulary or word frequency levels and thus can only provide limited information about a text. Using this formula, the passage from *The Hunger Games* in Figure 2.1 scores at the seventh-grade level, which is a reasonable estimate given that the content is suggested for middle school students.

Flesch–Kincaid Grade-Level Score

Another easily accessible tool for determining readability formulas can be found on the word processing software installed on your computer. Simply type in a passage from a text that you would like to assess for readability, then run the calculation. For example, Microsoft Word can report a Flesch–Kincaid grade-level score to approximate difficulty, using an algorithm that includes the average sentence length (ASL) and average number of syllables per word (ASW), the same elements used to calculate the Fry readability formula: $(0.39 \times ASL) + (11.8 \times ASW) - 15.59$ (Graesser, McNamara, & Louwerse, 2011, p. 42). This measure has a high correlation with the Fry readability graph.

The program will also report a Flesch reading ease score by assigning the text a number on a 100-point scale. On this scale, the higher the score, the easier the text is to read. This formula is more commonly used in business to determine the difficulty of workplace documents. Both the Flesch–Kincaid and Flesch reading ease formulas calculate using the same text characteristics, but the algorithms are weighted differently to ensure that easier texts are reported as a lower number for grade-level purposes and are reported as higher numbers when considering the relative ease of the text. The Flesch reading ease score for this paragraph is rated difficult at 37.4, and the Flesch–Kincaid grade-level score is 12.0. The passage from *The Hunger Games* in Figure 2.1 has a reading ease score of 70.7, meaning that it should be understood by students ages 13–15, and a Flesch–Kincaid grade-level score of 6.9.

ATOS

This computerized readability formula is used by Renaissance Learning to gauge texts used with the Accelerated Reader software. The name reflects the partnership between Renaissance Learning (formerly Advantage Learning Systems) and Touchstone Applied Science Associates (TASA), which developed the Degrees of Reading Power tests. The determination of the grade level of the words in a text uses *The Educator's Word Frequency Guide* (Zeno et al., 1995) at TASA. The ATOS formula computes words per sentence, average grade level of words, and characters per word, as measured by the entire text, not just sample passages. In addition, the formula factors whether the book is fiction or nonfiction (the latter is considered more difficult), and the length of the book (longer texts are more difficult). The developers of ATOS also state that emergent reading texts are further computed using Reading Recovery book levels to convert the formula into a guideline for primary teachers. Thus, *Wishy Washy Day* by Joy Cowley (1998) carries an ATOS level of 0.8, which translates to a Reading Recovery book level span of 6–9 (School Renaissance Institute, 2000).

Practical advantages of the ATOS measure include the large number of trade books in its database (140,000) and the free calculation service for measuring other texts, such as magazine articles and short stories. As with all readability formulas, the ATOS formula does not take content into consideration, so *The Catcher in the Rye* by J.D. Salinger (1951) carries a grade-level rating of 4.7. The makers caution that this measure should not be used in isolation, and each book also carries an interest-level measure to further guide educators, students, and parents. Therefore, the same text has an interest-level rating as upper grades (9–12). *The Hunger Games* earns a book-level measurement of 5.3 but an interest level of upper middle grades (6 and up).

Readability Formulas That Also Measure Readers

Conventional readability formulas do not factor in other elements that can influence difficulty, such as content. For example, a Flesch–Kincaid grade-level analysis on a 100-word passage from *Cat's Cradle* by Kurt Vonnegut (1963/1998), a decidedly adult satire of a world on the brink of apocalypse, reveals a score of 2.3 because the passage contains short, clipped dialogue. Although this is not a typical result, it highlights some shortcomings when relying on readability formulas alone without considering the content and the reader. In the 1980s and 1990s, two commercially available readability formulas were developed that attempted to account for content factors, however imperfectly, and to project estimated comprehension levels of students at each grade level.

Degrees of Reading Power

This widely used formula uses "sentence length, number of words not on an updated version of the Dale list, and average number of letters per word" (Gunning, 2003, p. 178). A review by Graesser, McNamara, and Louwerse (2011) found that both Degrees of Reading Power (DRP) and Lexile (discussed in the following section) correlate strongly with the Flesch–Kincaid readability measure. Gunning reports that DRP uses a variation of an older readability formula called the Bormuth. What sets the Bormuth apart is that it was the first formula to use cloze as a criterion measure. Whereas the DRP formula is proprietary, the Bormuth formula uses average word length (AWL), average sentence length (ASL), and average number of familiar words (AFL; defined as those words that appear on the Dale–Chall list of 3,000 words) as follows:

$$\text{Bormuth readability score} = 0.886593 - (AWL \times 0.03640) + (AFW \times 0.161911) - (ASL \times 0.21401) - (ASL \times 0.000577) - (ASL \times 0.000005)$$

A perceived advantage of the DRP is that it calculates a reader's performance with text difficulty using the same scale so educators can match readers and books. The DRP does not make readability scores of assessed texts publicly available, so we are unable to report the DRP level for the passage from *The Hunger Games* in Figure 2.1.

Lexile

This commercially available readability formula, developed by Smith, Stenner, Horabin, and Smith (1989), is used widely by testing companies and textbook and trade publishers to designate relative text difficulty among products. Similar to the DRP, the Lexile relies on a 2,000-point scale that is used to describe both the readers and the text, making it easier for teachers to match one to the other. Adams (2009) cautions that although the Lexile scale relies primarily on measures of sentence length and word frequency, frequency measures are problematic in that it is nearly impossible to distinguish among relative levels of difficulty in the middle of the list, thereby resulting in texts that have similar scores but differ widely in terms of difficulty. The Lexile score assigned to *The Hunger Games* is 810, which means that it would be of appropriate reading difficulty for students in fourth and fifth grades. As we have noted, however, many of the themes in the book are not appropriate for students at these grade levels.

Both the DRP and the Lexile scale rely on conventional text analysis algorithms, with one notable exception: They also measure students to pair texts with readers. Both measures apply a similar approach for assessing students, using cloze items within reading passages. By using the same scale, a teacher can quickly match a student's DRP or Lexile scale test score to a book. However, this can be problematic, as readability formulas in general are imperfect. To simply look at a single test score and then locate a number on the cover of a book overlooks the qualitative and reader-specific factors that should always be considered.

Lexile scale scores play a prominent role in the Common Core State Standards for English Language Arts document, and one element in particular has drawn much attention. As identified by Williamson (2006), citing a 350-point Lexile gap between 12th-grade texts and those used in college, the grade-level bands themselves have been realigned to absorb this gap beginning in grades 2 and 3 (see NGA & CCSSO, 2010, p. 8). The intent is to systematically raise the quantitative expectation of text complexity systematically from elementary school so students in high school are prepared for the kinds of reading necessary in college and in many careers. Like the original grade-band scale, there is some overlap both at the low and high ends of the Lexile ranges across grade levels. Since the 2010 publication of the Common Core State Standards, the text complexity grade bands have been widened and now include other quantitative readability measures, as can be seen in Table 2.1.

The readability formulas discussed in this chapter thus far vary somewhat in their algorithms and the factors they use to quantify a text. These formulas draw on characteristics that serve as approximations of overall difficulty: length of word, frequency of occurrence in the language, number of syllables, sentence length, or inclusion of words on a specific

Table 2.1 Text Complexity Grade Bands and Associated Readability Ranges

Grade Band	CCSS 2010 Lexile	Revised CCSS 2011 Lexile	ATOS	DRP	FK	SR	RM
K–1	N/A	N/A	N/A	N/A	N/A	N/A	N/A
2–3	450–790	420–820	2.75–5.14	42–54	1.98–5.34	0.05–2.48	3.53–6.13
4–5	770–980	740–1010	4.97–7.03	52–60	4.51–7.73	0.84–5.75	5.42–7.92
6–8	955–1155	925–1185	7.00–9.98	57–67	6.51–10.34	4.11–10.66	7.04–9.57
9–10	1080–1305	1050–1335	9.67–12.01	62–72	8.32–12.12	9.02–13.93	8.41–10.81
11–CCR	1215–1355	1185–1385	11.20–14.10	67–74	10.34–14.2	12.30–14.50	9.57–12

Note. CCSS = Common Core State Standards; Lexile = Lexile Framework (MetaMetrics); ATOS = Accelerated Reader (Renaissance Learning); DRP = Degrees of Reading Power (Questar); FK = Flesch-Kincaid; SR = Source Rater (Educational Testing Service); RM = Pearson Reading Maturity Metric (Pearson Education); CCR = college and career readiness. CCSS 2010 Lexile ranges from *Common Core State Standards for English Language Arts and Literacy in History/Social Studies, Science, and Technical Subjects: Appendix A: Research Supporting Key Elements of the Standards and Glossary of Key Terms* (p. 8), by National Governors Association Center for Best Practices & Council of Chief State School Officers, 2010, Washington, DC: Authors. CCSS 2011 Lexile and other readability ranges from "The Common Core State Standards: Supporting Districts and Teachers With Text Complexity" webinar (PowerPoint presentation p. 7) delivered January 26, 2012, by Council of Chief State School Officers and retrieved from www.ccsso.org/Resources/Digital_Resources/The_Common_Core_State_Standards_Supporting_Districts_and_Teachers_with_Text_Complexity.html.

word list, such as the Dale–Chall. Some of these formulas are better than others at predicting comprehension. We present a number of different formulas because they are each used, in varying degrees, in school systems, and informed practitioners should understand what a formula is and is not measuring. Having said that, most of the formulas account for about 50% of the variation in comprehension. The Lexile formula is better, predicting about 75% of the variation (for more information, see MetaMetrics, n.d.).

One concern raised by some educators and reading researchers is that these formulas primarily measure surface-level complexity but do not get at deeper levels of meaning that are necessary to read longer and more sophisticated texts (Davison & Kantor, 1982). A newer readability measure, called Coh-Metrix, attempts to look at the deeper structures of a text, especially in its ability to present ideas cohesively. These analyses have primarily been within the fields of linguistics, artificial intelligence, and computational linguistics (Graesser, McNamara, & Louwerse, 2011). With the advancement of newer tools of analysis, especially those that can parse texts at a fine-grained level, and those that account for cohesion (i.e., the relationship between given and new knowledge), a more complex method of computing readability includes aspects of both semantic and syntactic features. These methods are discussed in depth in the next section.

Measuring Coreference and Cohesion

With the advent of digitalized texts, quantitative measures of texts have become easier to score. These texts can be conveniently loaded into a webpage that calculates quantitative information using any number of algorithms. Importantly, the expansion of digitalized texts and more powerful computational tools makes it possible to measure entire texts rather than samples. In addition, a newer approach to understanding texts, called latent semantic analysis, offers a way to move beyond surface-level measures of word frequency and word and sentence length to mathematically measure how words and phrases connect with other words and phrases across a text (Landauer, McNamara, Dennis, & Kintsch, 2007). This measure also takes into account the amount of implicit knowledge needed to understand the relationships among words and ideas. For instance, the word *cup* is associated with other words, such as *fork* and *plate*, as well as *coffee, set the table,* and *wash the dishes,* even though these terms may not appear in the text. A latent semantic analysis forms a map, or matrix, of connections that are beyond a human's ability to detect and measure.

In addition to latent semantic analysis measures, computational linguistics researchers have sought to further quantify other elements of text, including parts of speech, text genre, psycholinguistic dimensions of words (e.g., their relative level of abstraction or concreteness), and propositional density (i.e., how a noun or phrase is linked to an agent, recipient, location, or object). These and other related measures work together to influence a text's coreference—the extent to which a word or phrase references similar words or phrases in the surrounding text. For instance, argument overlap "is the most robust measure of lexical co-referentiality in that it measures how often two sentences share common arguments (nouns, pronouns, and noun phrases)" (Crossley, Dufty, McCarthy, & McNamara, 2007, p. 199).

As a simple example, consider these two sentences:

> The bookshelves sagged under the weight of the heavy, dusty books. No one had checked out these books from the library for many years, as evidenced by the infrequent checkout dates on the cards in their lonely front pockets.

The word *library* locates the bookshelves and the books, and the word *their* coreferences *books* in both the first and second sentences. *Checked out* and *checkout* are different parts of speech, but they coreference each other because of proximity and agency. A latent semantic analysis of the same short passage might reveal that there are further relationships beyond the text, including *librarian, library card*, and the process needed to borrow and return a book. Taken together, latent semantic analysis, psycholinguistic measures, and coreferencing combine to contribute to a text's cohesion—that is, the number of its meaning relations. We are not speaking of the overarching meanings related to theme, main ideas, and such but rather to how syntax and semantics interact to develop a coherent message within and across sentences and paragraphs within the same text.

These deeper text structures defy a simple counting of words, syllables, and sentences. Coh-Metrix was developed through the University of Memphis to provide researchers with a means for measuring characteristics related to cohesion (Graesser, McNamara, & Kulikowich, 2011). This tool uses 64 indices that report on measures, or metrics, related to research on discourse, language, and cognition to assign text difficulty. The developers of Coh-Metrix explain that these indexes cluster into five major frameworks—"(1) *words*, (2) *syntax*, (3) the explicit *textbase*, (4) the *situation model* (sometimes called the mental model), and (5) the discourse *genre and rhetorical structure* (the type of discourse and its composition)" (p. 224)—and argue that this moves beyond the single dimension of readability in other formulas.

The Coh-Metrix tool is available online for free (cohmetrix.memphis .edu/cohmetrixpr/index.html) and requires a simple sign-up. The online tool reports on these five indexes for texts up to 15,000 words long. However, the resulting report requires a level of interpretation that requires extensive technical knowledge about linguistics and text analysis. Although this tool is not necessarily one that could be easily applied directly to the classroom, it offers promise for ways to quantify texts at deeper structural levels while still preserving the surface structure measures of conventional readability formulas that have proven to be useful. There are plans to simplify Coh-Metrix and establish a website that would provide instructional suggestions based on an analysis of submitted material. Perhaps the most valuable application of Coh-Metrix is in the authors' recommendations about the identification of texts across five dimensions, each addressing a specific purpose and reader (Graesser, McNamara, & Kulikowich, 2011):

1. *Challenging texts with associated explanations.* Some assigned texts are considerably beyond students' ability level. In such cases, students need

comments by a teacher, tutor, group, or computer that explains technical vocabulary and points of difficulty. Students are greatly stretched by exposure to difficult content, strategies, and associated explanations.

2. *Texts at the zone of proximal development.* Some assigned texts are slightly above the difficulty level that students can handle. These texts gently push the envelope—they are not too easy or too difficult, but just right.

3. *Easy texts to build self-efficacy.* Easy texts are assigned to build reading fluency and self-efficacy. Struggling readers can lose self-confidence, self-efficacy, and motivation when beset with a high density of texts that they can barely handle, if at all.

4. *A balanced diet of texts at varying difficulty.* Texts may be assigned according to a distribution of alternatives 1, 2, and 3 above, mostly in the zone of proximal development. The balanced diet benefits from exposure to challenging texts, texts that gradually push the envelope, and texts that build self-efficacy. This approach also includes texts in different genres.

5. *Texts tailored to develop particular reading components.* Texts may be assigned adaptively in a manner that is sensitive to the student's complex profile of reading components. The texts attempt to rectify particular reading deficits or to advance particular reading skills. (p. 232)

These recommendations challenge us to apply quantitative measures in ways that create a text gradient that not only considers the reading itself but also takes the reader and the learning context into account. This, however, has not been seen as the primary function of quantitative reading formulas, and their use and misuse have resulted in cautions and criticisms.

Cautions and Criticisms of Readability Formulas

Perhaps the most widespread criticism of quantitative reading formulas is that they have been used as a device to manipulate text to meet a fixed numerical value, regardless of its effect on the text itself. For example, publishers may remove or substitute words or phrases to lower the quantitative score but inadvertently make the reading more difficult. For example, signal words (e.g., *first, last*) and transitional phrases (e.g., *in conclusion*) add length to the sentence and can thereby raise the score. However, words and phrases like these actually assist the reader by helping him or her internally organize the information. In fact, from a qualitative perspective (discussed further in Chapter 3), a profusion of signal words alerts the teacher to the fact that a text is using an internal structure to scaffold the reader's understanding. Conversely, their removal can lower the readability score but end up making the text far less coherent. Higher readability scores do not automatically signal difficulty. Beck, McKeown, Omanson, and Pople (1984) have demonstrated that texts with higher levels of coherence and vocabulary are easier to comprehend than similar texts that have been stripped of these features.

Another criticism is the assumption that a lower readability score automatically results in a greater ease of learning. Lowering the readability of story problems has been shown to not have any achievement effect in mathematics (Paul, Nibbelink, & Hoover, 1986). This study involved more than 1,000 students in grades 3–6, and these findings have been similarly reported in other studies in mathematics (e.g., Hembree, 1992). However, as Wolf, Herman, and Dietel (2010) note, "If students do not understand the questions in an assessment because they don't understand academic language, inferences about students' knowledge and skills may be invalid" (p. 8). Thus, there are times when ensuring that students can access the text would be appropriate.

Informational texts that use a high degree of technical vocabulary related to a discipline may score much higher because of the relative rarity in the general corpus, with no way to account for their much more frequent use in a specific one. For example, science texts have technical vocabulary that is comparatively rare on word frequency lists but commonly used within a discipline (Cohen & Steinberg, 1983). The word *photosynthesis* would be rare when compared with all words but much more frequent in the field of life sciences. Therefore, a biology textbook might have a higher readability score because of the presence of such words despite the fact that the topic is deeply explored within its pages. *The Educator's Word Frequency Guide* (Zeno et al., 1995) was developed in part to address these discipline-specific concerns, and it provides an index of dispersion for the use of such words.

Readability for Early Readers

Quantitative reading formulas are notoriously unreliable for works designed for beginning readers. Hiebert and Martin (2001) note that unique characteristics of the emergent reader make issues of decodability, independent word recognition, and pattern mastery more specialized than a simple measure of readability can identify. In addition, the sentence structures for these materials may be very short, sometimes a single word, with heavy reliance on illustrations from which the reader can draw extensive support. For these reasons, most quantitative readability formulas do not report expected measures for texts designed for very young students, primarily kindergartners and first graders. Phrases, fragments, unconventional punctuation, and poems, which by nature often use single words, also do not yield useful readability scores.

Hiebert (2011) expresses concern about the impact of the Common Core State Standards' call for raising the level of text complexity for emergent and early readers. While agreeing that the overall difficulty of texts for older readers has decreased in past decades, she argues that the reverse is true in the primary grades:

> With respect to kindergarten, there were *no* kindergarten texts in core reading programs 50 or even 20 years ago. The difficulty levels of kindergarten texts in current core reading programs are comparable to those of first-grade texts in the 1980s. (p. 26)

She further states that the new Lexile scale for the end of grades 2 and 3 now stand at 450L–790L. The upper end of this scale was previously set as the approximate level for the end of fourth grade. We share the concerns that she raises about the further increase in readability levels at the early grades, especially when so many young students are already having difficulty. Although we believe overall that a staircase effect can be successfully achieved when purposefully applied over the course of a student's education, we agree that the first steps on this staircase need to be carefully scaled so the youngest readers successfully acquire the fundamentals of reading, which means that they are reading texts that allow for practice with decoding and fluency.

Conclusion

Since the early part of the 20th century, educators have sought ways to order or level texts through quantitative measures of readability. These formulas vary somewhat, but they primarily measure surface-level features of a text, especially focusing on word and sentence length, and frequency of word occurrence on a generated list. More recent developments utilize the availability of digitalized texts to analyze longer texts, not just samples. Most important, advances in computational linguistics, psychology, and artificial intelligence have opened the door to a new generation of analytic tools that provide a more fine-grained measure of the relationships of words to one another, and the mental models that are necessary to understand them. A summary of the readability formulas discussed in this chapter can be found in Table 2.2.

As with all measures, each can report accurately on some aspects, while other equally important elements remain untouched. For this reason, quantitative measures should be viewed as a first step, but by

Table 2.2 Summary of Quantitative Text Measures

Name	Purpose	Factors Used	Ease of Use	Notes
Advantage–TASA Open Standard	Assesses text difficulty	• Words per sentence • Grade level of words • Character length across entire text	• Easy • Free online calculator and extensive published booklist	Factors fiction/nonfiction and length of text
Coh-Metrix	Assesses texts on 64 indexes, including measures of text cohesion, linguistic elements, and parsers	• Parsers • Propositions • Latent semantic analysis • Traditional readability measures	• Easy • Online calculator	Reports require a high degree of technical knowledge to interpret
Degrees of Reading Power	Assesses text difficulty and reader skills using same scale	• Sentence length • Relative word frequency	• Hard • Proprietary software	Designed as criterion-referenced measures for use in grades 1–12
Flesch reading ease score	Assesses text difficulty	• Sentence length • Syllables	• Easy • Word-processing software	Reports relative ease as compared with students from grades 5 through college
Flesch–Kincaid grade-level score	Assesses text difficulty	• Sentence length • Syllables	• Easy • Word-processing software	For grades K–12
Fry readability formula	Assesses text difficulty	• Sentence length • Syllables	• Easy • Graph	For primary grades through college
Lexile scale	Assesses text difficulty and reader skills using same scale	• Sentence length • Relative word frequency	• Hard • Proprietary software	Reports as grade bands (grades 2+) and uses a similar scale to report student reading ability as measured by cloze items
New Dale–Chall readability formula	Assesses text difficulty	• Sentence length • Difficult words (i.e., those that do not appear on a list of 3,000 common words)	• Easy • Online calculator	For grades 4+

no means a final one, in determining the optimum text for a reader. Readability, after all, should never be confused with reading ability. In the next chapters, we will explore another necessary element for determining text complexity: qualitative analysis.

REFERENCES

Adams, M.J. (2009). The challenge of advanced texts: The interdependence of reading and learning. In E.H. Hiebert (Ed.), *Reading more, reading better* (pp. 163–189). New York: Guilford.

Anderson, R.C., Hiebert, E.H., Scott, J.A., & Wilkinson, I.A.G. (1985). *Becoming a nation of readers: The report of the Commission on Reading.* Champaign, IL: Center for the Study of Reading; Washington, DC: National Academy of Education, National Institute of Education.

Beck, I.L., McKeown, M.G., Omanson, R.C., & Pople, M.T. (1984). Improving the comprehensibility of stories: The effects of revisions that improve coherence. *Reading Research Quarterly, 19*(3), 263–277.

Chall, J.S., & Dale, E. (1995). *Manual for the new Dale-Chall readability formula.* Cambridge, MA: Brookline.

Cohen, S.A., & Steinberg, J.E. (1983). Effects of three types of vocabulary on readability of intermediate grade science textbooks: An application of Finn's transfer feature theory. *Reading Research Quarterly, 19*(1), 86–101.

Council of Chief State School Officers. (2012, January 26). *The Common Core State Standards: Supporting districts and teachers with text complexity* [Webinar]. Wasington, DC: Author. Retrieved from www.ccsso.org/Resources/Digital_ Resources/The_Common_Core_State_Standards_Supporting_Districts_and_ Teachers_with_Text_Complexity.html

Crossley, S.A., Dufty, D.F., McCarthy, P.M., & McNamara, D.S. (2007). Toward a new readability: A mixed model approach. In D.S. McNamara & J.G. Trafton (Eds.), *Proceedings of the 29th annual conference of the Cognitive Science Society* (pp. 197– 202). Austin, TX: Cognitive Science Society.

Dale, E., & O'Rourke, J. (1976). *The living word vocabulary, the words we know: A national vocabulary inventory.* Elgin, IL: Dome.

Davison, A., & Kantor, R.N. (1982). On the failure of readability formulas to define readable texts: A case study from adaptations. *Reading Research Quarterly, 17*(2), 187–209.

Fry, E. (2002). Readability versus leveling. *The Reading Teacher, 56*(3), 286–291.

Graesser, A.C., McNamara, D.S., & Kulikowich, J.M. (2011). Coh-Metrix: Providing multilevel analyses of text characteristics. *Educational Researcher, 40*(5), 223–234. doi:10.3102/0013189X11413260

Graesser, A.C., McNamara, D.S., & Louwerse, M.M. (2011). Methods of automated text analysis. In M.L. Kamil, P.D. Pearson, E.B. Moje, & P.P. Afflerbach (Eds.), *Handbook of reading research* (Vol. IV, pp. 34–53). New York: Routledge.

Gray, W.S., & Leary, B.E. (1935). *What makes a book readable, with special reference to adults of limited reading ability: An initial study.* Chicago: University of Chicago Press.

Gunning, T.G. (2003). The role of readability in today's classrooms. *Topics in Language Disorders, 23*(3), 175–189. doi:10.1097/00011363-200307000-00005

Hembree, R. (1992). Experiments and relational studies in problem solving: A meta-analysis. *Journal for Research in Mathematics Education, 23*(3), 242–273.

Hiebert, E.H. (2011). The Common Core's staircase of text complexity: Getting the size of the first step right. *Reading Today, 29*(3), 26–27.

Hiebert, E.H., & Martin, L.A. (2001). The texts of beginning reading instruction. In S.B. Neuman & D.K. Dickinson (Eds.), *Handbook of early literacy research* (pp. 361–376). New York: Guilford.

Just, M.A., & Carpenter, P.A. (1992). A capacity theory of comprehension: Individual differences in working memory. *Psychological Review, 99*(1), 122–149. doi:10.1037/0033-295X.99.1.122

Kintsch, W. (with Crothers, E.J. et al.). (1974). *The representation of meaning in memory.* Hillsdale, NJ: Erlbaum.

Landauer, T.K., McNamara, D.S., Dennis, S., & Kintsch W. (Eds.). (2007). *Handbook of latent semantic analysis.* Mahwah, NJ: Erlbaum.

MetaMetrics. (n.d.). *What does the Lexile® measure mean?* Durham, NC: Author. Retrieved January 8, 2012, from www.lexile.com/m/uploads/downloadablepdfs/WhatDoestheLexileMeasureMean.pdf

National Governors Association Center for Best Practices & Council of Chief State School Officers. (2010). *Common Core State Standards for English language arts and literacy in history/social studies, science, and technical subjects: Appendix A: Research supporting key elements of the standards and glossary of key terms.* Washington, DC: Authors.

Paul, D.J., Nibbelink, W.H., & Hoover, H.D. (1986). The effects of adjusting readability on the difficulty of mathematics story problems. *Journal for Research in Mathematics Education, 17*(3), 163–171.

School Renaissance Institute. (2000). *The ATOS™ readability formula for books and how it compares to other formulas.* Madison, WI: Author. Retrieved January 3, 2011, from www.windsorct.org/sagelmc/ReadabilityComparisonArticle.pdf

Smith, D.R., Stenner, A.J., Horabin, I., & Smith, M. (1989). *The Lexile scale in theory and practice: Final report.* Durham, NC: MetaMetrics. (ERIC Document Reproduction Service No. ED307577)

Wikipedia. (2011). *Brown corpus.* Retrieved January 3, 2011, from en.wikipedia.org/wiki/Brown_Corpus

Williamson, G.L. (2006). *Aligning the journey with the destination: A model for K–16 reading standards.* Durham, NC: MetaMetrics.

Wolf, M.K., Herman, J.L., & Dietel, R. (2010). *Improving the validity of English language learner assessment systems: Full policy brief* (CRESST Policy Brief No. 10). Los Angeles: National Center for Research on Evaluation, Standards, & Student Testing, University of California. Retrieved January 3, 2011, from www.cse.ucla.edu/products/policy/PolicyBrief10_FRep_ELLPolicy.pdf

Zeno, S.M., Ivens, S.H., Millard, R.T., & Duvvuri, R. (1995). *The educator's word frequency guide.* Brewster, NY: Touchstone Applied Science Associates.

LITERATURE CITED

Cisneros, S. (1991). Eleven. In *Woman hollering creek and other stories* (pp. 6–9). New York: Vintage.

Collins, S. (2008). *The hunger games.* New York: Scholastic.

Cowley, J. (1998). *Wishy washy day.* Chicago: Wright Group.

Salinger, J.D. (1951). *The catcher in the rye.* Boston: Little, Brown.

Vonnegut, K. (1998). *Cat's cradle.* New York: Delta. (Original work published 1963)

CHAPTER 3

Qualitative Measures of Text Complexity

Qualitative dimensions and qualitative factors refer to those aspects of text complexity best measured or only measurable by an attentive human reader, such as levels of meaning or purpose; structure; language conventionality and clarity; and knowledge demands.

—NGA & CCSSO, 2010, p. 4

*B*ug is a fairly easy word. Most students have background knowledge about bugs and know the label for the concept of bug. The word itself would not cause readers much trouble, and readability formulas would not indicate that there were problems with the difficulty of this word. Yet, consider the following sentences and how *bug* is used:

- When I saw the bug, I screamed for help.
- When I saw the Bug, I remembered my first car.
- When I saw the bug, I wondered who was spying on me.

Sometimes there are words, or ideas, that throw off the reader but are not picked up by readability formulas. It takes a human to notice these aspects of text difficulty, and the architects of the Common Core State Standards recognized this, as evidenced in the quote that opens this chapter.

As Bailin and Grafstein (2001) noted, readability formulas are

both seductive and misleading: seductive, because the application of a mathematical formula lends an aura of scientific objectivity to the number derived from it, and misleading, because the apparent objectivity of the score lulls naïve educators or librarians into having greater confidence in it than they would in their own informal judgements, and certainly more than is warranted by the evidence. (p. 292)

We agree that readability formulas are seductive and can be misleading, and we think that speed of assessment is the reason that they have been used for nearly 100 years (Lively & Pressey, 1923). The formulas are fast and reasonably accurate at identifying levels of texts for a specific reader in three broad areas: frustration, instruction, and independence. When looking at a large number of texts, readability formulas can help narrow the selections for students reading at a specific grade level. What quantitative measures of readability are not very good at include things that a human reader needs to notice. The president of MetaMetrics, the company that produces the Lexile framework, noted this in an interview:

> While a Lexile measure is a valuable piece of information in the book-selection process, it's important to note that the Lexile measure is only one piece of information to consider when selecting a book for a specific student. Other factors, such as the content and quality of the text, and the student's interests and reading goals, should also be considered. (Harvey, 2011, p. 59)

Considerate Texts

As we noted in Chapter 1, there has been research on qualitative factors that make texts more or less difficult to read and understand (e.g., Armbruster, 1984; Baumann, 1986; Konopak, 1988). The overarching terms for this research are *considerate texts* or *friendly texts* (Anderson & Armbruster, 1984; Dreher & Singer, 1989). These are texts that facilitate comprehension and learning because the texts are, or have been written to be, responsive to readers. There are three overlapping features of text that contribute to comprehension and learning: structure, coherence, and audience appropriateness (e.g., Boscolo & Mason, 2003; Kobayashi, 2002; Meyer, 2003).

In terms of structure, there is significant evidence that the manner in which the ideas or topics are arranged and related impacts students' comprehension (Bakken & Whedon, 2002; Ciardiello, 2002; Parsons, 2000). The most common informational text structures include (Fisher & Frey, 2012):

- *Description:* A list of information
- *Compare and contrast:* Noted similarities and differences between two concepts
- *Temporal sequence:* How events change or remain the same over time

- *Cause and effect:* Causal relationships
- *Problem and solution:* S situation or issue and how it is resolved

The common narrative text structure is story grammar, which includes plot-driven narratives that involve characters, dialogue, conflicts, and resolutions. Students in the primary grades recognize story structure because it is commonly used in storytelling (McCabe & Rollins, 1994). Narrative texts can also use some of the more informational text structures noted previously. For example, *There Was an Old Lady Who Swallowed a Fly* by Simms Taback (1997) is fiction for young children told as a sequence story. Understanding that it is fiction, has a plot structure, and is told in backward chronological order helps kindergartners understand the text.

There are a number of text features that authors and editors can use to create a more considerate text (Dreher & Singer, 1989; Flood, Mathison, Lapp, & Singer, 1989). For example, headings and subheadings can guide readers through information. Also, signal words that convey the structure (e.g., *first, second,* and *third* for description; *because, since,* or *as a result* for cause and effect) can help students process information. Similarly, margin notes and graphic organizers, such as Venn diagrams, structured overviews, semantic feature analyses, and maps, can provide readers with an alternative way to understand the information being presented.

The second factor that ensures that texts are considerate of their readers relates to the idea that concepts, phenomena, and events can be developed and explained in a logical and straightforward manner. This concept is known as coherence—a systematic or logical connection or consistency within the text. As with structure, there is significant evidence that coherence is an important consideration in the readability of a text (McNamara & Kintsch, 1996; Meyer, 2003; Sanders, 1997).

Like structure, there are a number of ways that authors and editors can specifically address the issue of text coherence. First, when main ideas are explicitly stated and in an obvious place as they start each section, readers are more likely to understand the information. Second, when the information found within a paragraph or section is clearly connected back to the main idea, coherence is improved. Third, when there is a logical order of events and obvious relationships between events and topics, comprehension is easier and more likely to occur. Fourth, when readers are provided with clear references and referents, and ambiguous pronouns are avoided, texts are easier to understand. Finally, when there are smooth transitions between topics, reading is smooth and feels comfortable. These are all significant factors to consider when analyzing a text and its ability to engage readers and maintain their attention (Lapp & Flood, 1982).

The final factor that makes a text considerate highlights the extent to which the material corresponds with the knowledge of the intended audience. In other words, audience appropriateness is a measure of how well the text matches the students' probable background and prior knowledge (Fisher & Frey, 2009). These are two important factors for consideration. Some writers consider how much information their readers already know, and can then "elaborate new concepts sufficiently to be meaningful to readers and to facilitate learning" (Armbruster, 1996, p. 54). The research on audience appropriateness is particularly strong (Alexander, Schallert, & Hare, 1991; Fisher, Ross, & Grant, 2010; Seda, Ligouri, & Seda, 1999) and clearly indicates that this is a powerful factor in creating considerate texts.

As with structure and coherence, there are a number of ways that authors can choose to address the issue of audience appropriateness. First, they can evaluate the conceptual density (i.e., the number of new concepts per unit of text) to ensure that there is not a significant overload of new information all at once. Second, they can introduce new content by making connections with what the reader already knows. Third, they can provide more information about fewer topics, thus allowing a precise focus on the content under investigation. In doing so, the text use validates and extends the information that students already have about a topic. Fourth, the text can specifically address the common misconceptions that readers have. These misconceptions are often the source of audience mismatch, as students may not be able to integrate new information unless their misunderstandings are specifically addressed.

But Not All Texts Are Considerate

The extensive research completed on considerate texts has resulted in a deep understanding of the qualitative factors that influence text complexity. The challenge is that all texts are not created considerately. Although textbooks can be created to be considerate of their readers, and many magazines use the idea of considerate text to keep their subscription rates high, many of the texts worthy of reading violate one or more of the factors identified previously (Flood, 1986). Consider the preamble to the U.S. Constitution, arguably one of our nation's more important documents. It's not very considerate, at least by today's standards:

> We the People of the United States, in Order to form a more perfect Union, establish Justice, insure domestic Tranquility, provide for the common defence, promote the general Welfare, and secure the Blessings of Liberty to ourselves and our Posterity, do ordain and establish this Constitution for the United States of America.

Yet, it is worthy of understanding. A more considerate version could be used in the classroom, which has been an unintended consequence of the research on considerate texts. In an effort to ensure that students were able to understand what they read, publishers were encouraged to produce texts that met all of the criteria for considerateness, thereby removing the struggle that is so important in developing reading habits.

The Common Core State Standards challenge these assumptions. Instead of providing students with an alternative version of the Constitution's preamble, for example, teachers have to understand why the text is hard and then teach students how to read it. Struggling with the ideas in the preamble, such as who is we, why are some words capitalized, what is domestic tranquility, and why it is more perfect and not perfect, is really important. There are so many things worth talking about when you've read a piece of text worthy of focus. Our example is the preamble to the U.S. Constitution, but it could have just as easily been Franz Kafka's (1946) *Metamorphosis*:

> When Gregor Samsa woke up one morning from unsettling dreams, he found himself changed in his bed into a monstrous vermin. He was lying on his back as hard as armor plate, and when he lifted his head a little, he saw his vaulted brown belly, sectioned by arch-shaped ribs, to whose dome the cover, about to slide off completely, could barely cling. His many legs, pitifully thin compared with the size of the rest of him, were waving helplessly before his eyes. (p. 3)

Again, that's not to say that we should drop the Constitution's preamble or some existential reading, such as Kafka's *Metamorphosis*, on student desks and tell them to read and understand it independently; we have to do a lot of teaching to scaffold student understanding. We should also not simply replace the texts we invite students to read with easier, or more considerate, versions. This Kafka passage is difficult, especially because it takes a while to realize that Gregor has been transformed into an insect, but it is essential to the appreciation of this landmark piece of literature that it slowly dawns on us that Gregor is horribly changed.

As we have noted, the research on considerate text has resulted in a deep understanding of qualitative factors that make text hard for readers to understand. These factors can be used to identify which texts can and should be selected for use in the classroom. In the Common Core State Standards, there are specific areas of note related to qualitative factors, including levels of meaning and purpose, structure, language conventionality and clarity, and knowledge demands. We explore these four topics next. A rubric for qualitatively analyzing narrative and informational texts can be found in Figure 3.1.

When using this scale for a quick assessment of a reader–text match, we give each category a score from 3 (stretch) to 1 (comfortable). Scoring the text provides a quick composite overview of the areas that need instruction. For example, when several ninth graders wanted to form a book club to read *I Am Nujood, Age 10 and Divorced* by Nujood Ali (2010), their teacher realized by quickly glancing at this scale that the only areas in which the readers–text match would receive a score of 3 (stretch) was in the subcategories identified within the major section of knowledge demands. Further analysis of the subcategories helped craft an initial instructional conversation with this group that involved discussing the location, history, customs, religion, and cultural beliefs of Yemen and the Middle East regarding the marriage of young girls. With this as a base of introductory knowledge, these students were then able to enjoy their book club text and create a shared blog, which included drawings and photos illustrating their interpretations of the courage they felt was shown by Nujood through her story of defiance.

Similarly, when a third-grade teacher evaluated *Throw Your Tooth on the Roof: Tooth Traditions From Around the World* by Selby Beeler (1998), she determined that although the quantitative reading measure would be accessible for most of her students, other factors contributed to its complexity. The diverse geographic locations and some unfamiliar cultures made the text more demanding in regard to background

Figure 3.1 Qualitative Measures of Text Complexity Rubric

Score	3 points (Stretch): Texts That Would Stretch a Reader and/or Require Instruction	2 points (Grade Level): Texts That Require Grade-Appropriate Skills	1 point (Comfortable): Texts That Are Comfortable and/or Build Background, Fluency, and Skills
Levels of Meaning and Purpose			
Density and complexity	Significant density and complexity, with multiple levels of meaning; meanings may be more ambiguous	Single but more complex or abstract level of meaning; some meanings are stated, whereas others are left to the reader to identify	Single and literal levels of meaning; meaning is explicitly stated
Figurative language	Plays a significant role in identifying the meaning of the text; more sophisticated figurative language used (e.g., irony and satire, allusions, archaic or less familiar symbolism); reader left to interpret these meanings	Imagery, metaphors, symbolism, personification, and so forth used to make connections within the text to more explicit information; readers supported in understanding these language devices through examples and explanations	Limited use of symbolism, metaphors, and poetic language that allude to other unstated concepts; language explicit and relies on literal interpretations
Purpose	Deliberately withheld from the reader, who must use other interpretative skills to identify it	Implied but easily identified based on the title or context	Directly and explicitly stated at the beginning of the reading
Structure			
Genre	Unfamiliar or bends and expands the rules for the genre	Unfamiliar but is a reasonable example of the genre or familiarly bends and expands the rules for the genre	Familiar and text consistent with the elements of the genre
Organization	Distorts time or sequence in a deliberate effort to delay the reader's full understanding of the plot, process, or set of concepts; may include significant flashbacks, foreshadowing, or shifting perspectives	Adheres to most conventions but digresses on occasion to temporarily shift the reader's focus to another point of view, event, time, or place before returning to the main idea or topic	Conventional, sequential, or chronological, with clear signals and transitions to lead the reader through a story, process, or set of concepts
Narration	Unreliable narrator provides a distorted or limited view to the reader; the reader must use other clues to deduce the truth; multiple narrators provide conflicting information; shifting points of view keep the reader guessing.	Third-person limited or first person narration provides accurate but limited perspectives or viewpoints.	Third-person omniscient narration or an authoritative and credible voice provides an appropriate level of detail and keeps little hidden from the view of the reader.
Text features and graphics	Limited use to organize information and guide the reader; information in the graphics not repeated in the main part of the text but essential for understanding the text	Wider array that competes for the reader's attention (e.g., margin notes, diagrams, graphs, font changes); graphics and visuals used to augment and illustrate information in the main part of the text	Organize information explicitly and guide the reader (e.g., bold and italicized words, headings and subheadings); maybe graphics or illustrations present, but not necessary to understand the main part of the text

(continued)

Figure 3.1 Qualitative Measures of Text Complexity Rubric (continued)

Score	3 points (Stretch): Texts That Would Stretch a Reader and/or Require Instruction	2 points (Grade Level): Texts That Require Grade-Appropriate Skills	1 point (Comfortable): Texts That Are Comfortable and/or Build Background, Fluency, and Skills
		Language Conventionality and Clarity	
Standard English and variations	Includes significant and multiple styles of English and its variations, which are unfamiliar to the reader	Some distance between the reader's linguistic base and the language conventions used in the text; vernacular unfamiliar to the reader	Closely adheres to the reader's linguistic base
Register	Archaic, formal, domain-specific, or scholarly	Consultative or formal, and may be academic but acknowledges the developmental level of the reader	Casual and familiar
		Knowledge Demands	
Background knowledge	Demands on the reader that extend far beyond one's experiences; provides little in the way of explanation of these divergent experiences	Distance between the reader's experiences and those in the text, but acknowledgment of these divergent experiences and sufficient explanation to bridge these gaps	Content that closely matches the reader's life experiences
Prior knowledge	Specialized or technical content knowledge presumed; little review or explanation of these concepts present in the text	Subject-specific knowledge required but augmented with review or summary of this information	Needed to understand that the text is familiar and draws on a solid foundation of practical, general, and academic learning
Cultural knowledge	Relies on extensive or unfamiliar intertextuality and uses artifacts and symbols that reference archaic or historical cultures.	Primarily references contemporary and popular culture to anchor explanations for new knowledge; intertextuality used more extensively but mostly familiar to the reader	The reader uses familiar cultural templates to understand the text; limited or familiar intertextuality
Vocabulary	Demand is extensive, domain-specific, and representative of complex ideas; little offered in the way of context clues to support the reader	Draws on domain-specific, general academic, and multiple-meaning words, with text supports to guide the reader's correct interpretations of their meanings; represents familiar concepts and ideas	Controlled and uses the most commonly held meanings; multiple-meaning words used in a limited fashion

knowledge and cultural knowledge. Also, the overall organization of the book is comparative, with discussions of how the loss of a deciduous tooth is addressed in many societies. Based on her assessment, the teacher provided additional instruction as needed on unfamiliar cultures and locations. Importantly, she assisted her students in understanding the meta-organizational structure of the text by creating a class chart divided into continents. As they read about tooth traditions in Mexico, Cameroon, and Russia, the students composed notes about each, then consulted an atlas to determine the correct continent. This codeveloped chart provided the teacher with a tool to find similarities and differences within regions, a point implied but not explicitly stated in the book.

We do not intend this scale to be used as if it were scientifically calibrated; rather, we share it as we use it, for a quick check that helps us assess a reader–text match. This information informs our planning of instruction designed to support the student's reading of the targeted text. We believe that with the appropriate instructional supports, any text is within the reach of the reader.

Levels of Meaning and Purpose

Some texts can be taken at face value, whereas others are more like onions, with layer upon layer of meaning. A literal reading of *Animal Farm* by George Orwell (1946), in which animals take over the farm and begin to rule themselves, is very different from a reading in which the reader understands the metaphors being used to describe Russia. For example, the Battle of the Cowshed is a metaphor for the overthrow of the old Russian government based on tsars. The same range of levels of meaning can be found in picture books, chapter books, and trade books. For example, in *Cat and Mouse* by Tomasz Bogacki (1996), the literal story focuses on a cat family and a mouse family and how they became friends. Yet, the deeper meaning focuses on what children are taught and how they can develop friendships with people who are different from them. Similarly, *Petey* by Ben Mikaelsen (1998) is literally about a person with a disability who lives in an institution, but there are layers of meaning related to how that society treats people with disabilities and what it means to have friends and advocate on behalf of them.

Density and Complexity

To qualitatively analyze the level of a text's meaning is difficult. In some cases, the text is dense and complex, whereas in other cases, the text is literal and explicit. Straightforward texts that provide rich descriptions are less complex than those that are ambiguous or require extensive inferences. That's not to say that direct and straightforward texts are better than those that require meaning making. There are a number of fantastic texts that are worth the work required to understand them. It's just that teachers should know why these texts are complex, if they are appropriate for the students in the classroom, and how they might best be taught. Returning to *Animal Farm*, in the "Beasts of England" song, Orwell does not come right out and say that people are going to be free from the harnesses and restraints of the government. This excerpt from the song takes some work to understand because the layers of meaning are complex, and the author does not explicitly say what he means:

> Soon or late the day is coming,
> Tyrant Man shall be o'erthrown,
> And the fruitful fields of England
> Shall be trod by beasts alone.
>
> Rings shall vanish from our noses,
> And the harness from our back,
> Bit and spur shall rust forever,
> Cruel whips no more shall crack. (pp. 9–10)

Figurative Language

In addition to density and complexity, figurative language can make a text more complex. When authors use irony, idioms, metaphor, symbolism, or other literary devices, the reader has to think a little more. When these are not used, the text is easier to understand.

Consider the work of Dr. Seuss. He uses symbolism often, which makes his books harder than they might otherwise seem to be. For example, Dr. Seuss reflects on fascism in "Yertle the Turtle" (1958), friendship and otherness in "The Sneetches" (1961), environmentalism in *The Lorax* (1971), and commercialism in *How the Grinch Stole Christmas* (1957). It's not that figurative language is reserved for complex poetry but rather that it is all around us. When we understand figurative language, it makes the reading more interesting because our minds get a chance to work. Having said that, when we do not grasp the figurative language, we miss a lot of the text's meaning.

If the reader does not think deeply about the metaphorical connection between a stage and life itself, he or she is not likely to understand this passage from William Shakespeare's (2009) *As You Like It*:

> All the world's a stage
> And all the men and women merely players:
> They have their exits and their entrances
> And one man in his time plays many parts (p. 140)

See Table 3.1 for a list of common literary devices.

Table 3.1 Common Literary Devices

Device	Explanation
Allegory	A story that is used to teach something (e.g., parables in the Bible, Aesop's fables). The stories are usually long and require analysis to find the allegory or intention.
Alliteration	Occurs when the author uses the same letter or sound to start each word in a string (e.g., "Andrea anxiously awaited arrangement"); used frequently in books for emergent readers in part to foster phonemic awareness
Allusion	A reference to a well-known person, myth, historical event, biblical story, etc. (e.g., "she's just like Narcissus," "it's as bad as the sinking of the *Titanic*")
Flashback	Pauses the action to comment on or portray a scene that took place earlier (e.g., during a scene in which a person walks through a dark alley, the author pauses to relate a story about another time when the character was scared)
Foreshadowing	A hint of things to come—usually, but not always, an unpleasant event
Hyperbole	An exaggerated comment or line used for effect and not meant to be taken literally (e.g., "when faced with a long line at the Department of Motor Vehicles, Andrew said, 'It will take an eternity to be allowed to drive'")
Imagery	Involves language that evokes one or all of the five senses: sight, hearing, taste, smell, and/or touching (e.g., "her lips taste of honey and dew," "walking through the halls, amid the crashing sound of lockers closing and the smell of yesterday's coffee, I saw the radiant teacher")

(continued)

Table 3.1 Common Literary Devices (continued)

Device	Explanation
Irony and satire	Use of sophisticated humor to relay a message, often saying what something is when the opposite or reverse could be true; irony used to say one thing when the author means another (e.g., "Looking at the shark bite in his surfboard, James says, 'Finally, I've got a short board'"); satire used to focus more on mockery or wit to attack or ridicule something
Metaphor	Make a direct comparison without using *like* or *as*; simply makes a comparison in which one thing is said to be another (e.g., "the dog's fur was electric, standing on end in fear")
Personification	When authors give animals, ideas, or actions the qualities of humans; common in Disney films and children's books; also used for more abstract ideas (e.g., "hate has you trapped in her arms")
Point of view	First person: story told from the perspective of the narrator, and the reader cannot know or witness anything that the narrator does not tell; second person: narrator speaks directly to the reader (e.g., "you will likely know by now that Andre is a bad guy"); third person: narrator omniscient (all-knowing) and can convey different perspectives at different times
Simile	A comparison using *like* or *as* (e.g., "like a rain-filled cloud, Anna cried and cried when she learned of her lost fortune")
Symbolism	An object or action that means something more than its literal meaning (e.g., a black crow in the text prepares readers for death; the sighting of a white dove conveys peace or life)
Tone and mood	The attitude an author takes toward a subject or character (e.g., hateful, serious, humorous, sarcastic, solemn, objective) through the use of dialogue, settings, or descriptions

Note. The use and understanding of literary devices allows students to understand texts and share conversations with their peers about texts using common terms. Further, as students understand increasingly complex literary devices and read them in texts, they will begin to use these devices in their writing, thus making their writing come alive.

Purpose

The purpose of the text also impacts text complexity qualitatively. Some texts have subtle purposes, whereas others have explicitly stated purposes. Sometimes the author states the purpose as a main idea right up front, and other times the reader is left to figure out why the author wrote the specific text and what the author wants the reader to know or do with the information. The role of purpose can be easily highlighted by comparing a textbook that starts each section with a clear purpose and main idea statement with a fable such as "The Boy Who Cried Wolf," in which the purpose has to be inferred. It's not just that informational texts have a purpose, and narrative texts do not. There is a wide range of informational texts that do not have an explicitly stated purpose, such as *Animal Disguises* by Belinda Weber (2004). It's clear that this book provides information for the reader and is very interesting, but it does not come right out and tell the reader what the purpose is and what to expect. As such, the text is a little more complex than a book that explicitly says something like, "In this section, we focus on camouflage as one of the ways that animals can disguise themselves."

We are not suggesting that having a clear purpose is a bad thing. When we want students to read and understand a textbook focused on U.S. history, it helps when they know the text's purpose. It's also important to recognize that not all texts have a clearly stated purpose and that we have to recognize the complexity of those texts and teach students how to read them.

Structure

As we noted in the section on considerate texts, there are structures that writers use to convey their ideas. As with other factors that make texts complex, these structures are sometimes simple and explicit and other times complex and implicit. Again, there is no value judgment placed on the text itself. Simple and explicit is not necessarily better than complex and implicit. Rather, understanding what makes a text complex and how to help students understand the text must be our goals as educators.

Genre

Readers should recognize the genre of the text. Although there are debates about what makes a genre, most people agree that literature in the same genre has similarities in form and style. At the global level, readers should know if they are reading fiction or nonfiction. From there, they should recognize genres of texts, such as those found in Figure 3.2. At a more discrete level, readers should recognize subgenres and traits that are specific to a certain discipline (Shanahan & Shanahan, 2008). For example, historical texts include primary and secondary sources. Whereas other types of texts use references, sourcing is especially important in history.

Figure 3.2 Genre Wheel

LIVED LIVES
- Biography
- Autobiography
- Memoir

NEW FORMS
- Graphic novels
- Sequential arts
- e-zines
- Blogs
- Wikis
- Fanfiction

ARCHETYPES
- Fables
- Folktales
- Myths
- Legends

CHARACTER AND PLOT
- Historical fiction
- Realistic fiction
- Mystery

READ TO LEARN ABOUT

- Poetry
- Haiku
- Epics
- Lyrical poetry
- Song lyrics
- Plays
- Podcasts

- Science fiction
- Fantasy

SPOKEN WORD

ALTERNATIVE UNIVERSES

- Informational text
- News magazines
- Newspapers
- Technical

- Comparative essays
- Editorial
- Position piece
- Advertisements
- Propaganda

THE WORLD AROUND YOU

RHETORIC AND OPINION

Note. From *Background Knowledge: The Missing Piece of the Comprehension Puzzle* (p. 104), by D. Fisher and N. Frey, 2009, Portsmouth, NH: Heinemann. Copyright 2009 by Douglas Fisher and Nancy Frey. Reprinted with permission.

In science, different or alternative representations (e.g., pictures, graphs, charts, text, diagrams) of an idea are essential for a full understanding of the concepts.

In part, genre influences text difficulty because of students' experiences. If students have a lot of experiences with realistic fiction, for example, then another book in that genre will be easier for them to manage. Alternatively, if they have not had a lot of experience with persuasive speeches, then understanding Martin Luther King's "I have a dream" speech will be more difficult. This is particularly important in elementary schools because young students have limited experience with informational texts (Duke, 2000). Although the Common Core State Standards call for a balance of informational and narrative texts, many students do not have experience with the range of genres available. As such, some texts are more difficult than others simply because students have been undertaught the conventions or style of the particular genre.

Organization

Additionally, the text should be assessed qualitatively for its organization. If the organization is conventional, with main ideas clearly stated or, in the case of narrative text, a predictable flow of events, then the text is likely to be easier for students to understand. Generally, texts organized in chronological order are less complex than those that use some other organizational pattern. In narrative texts, the use of flashbacks and foreshadowing make the text harder because of the shifts in time. The same is true for informational texts. When an author violates our understanding of chronology, we have to work harder to understand.

Further, if a text has an unconventional organizational pattern, such as is the case with *Voices in the Park* by Anthony Browne (1998), in which each section is a different voice (person) telling about the same event, and the fonts also differ, the text is harder to understand. The organizational conventions apply to narrative and informational texts, although each has its own conventions. For narrative texts, the organization typically follows a typical plot structure as outlined by Freytag (see Figure 3.3), including exposition (i.e., introduction to the theme, setting, characters, and circumstances), rising action, conflict, climax, falling action, and resolution. When a narrative text does not follow this convention, as is the case in "An Upheaval" by Anton Chekhov (1999), in which the exposition occurs throughout the short story and there is no resolution, readers have a harder time understanding it.

Informational texts are typically organized by one of the structures presented earlier, such as problem and solution. When this is the case, and readers have experiences with the structure, the reading is more comfortable. When authors violate the structure or do not present a main idea for the information they share, readers have to work a little harder.

Figure 3.3 Freytag's Pyramid

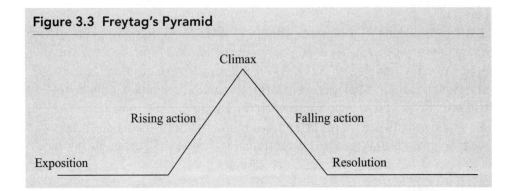

Inside the Titanic by Ken Marschall and Hugh Brewster (1997) provides readers with information in chronological order, with clear timelines and information. This text is easier to read than *Bury the Dead: Tombs, Corpses, Mummies, Skeletons, and Rituals* by Christopher Sloan (2002), even though it also has a timeline. The timeline in *Bury the Dead* stretches over thousands of years and crosses many continents, whereas *Inside the Titanic* focuses on a shorter period in history and one idea. Both are great books worthy of reading, but one is harder than the other, based on the organization used.

Narration

Another consideration related to the structure of the text is narration. If the point of view shifts in a narrative text, it's likely that the text will be harder for students to grasp. For example, in *Rose Blanche*, Roberto Innocenti (1985) starts with first-person narrative, using statements such as "My name is Rose Blanche. I live in a small town in Germany with narrow streets, old fountains and tall houses with pigeons on the roofs" (p. 1). Later in the book, the author shifts to third person, and the reader is left to infer what happened to the main character.

Similarly, some authors provide narrators for their stories. These can be first-, second-, or third-person narrators, and they can be limited or omniscient narrators. For many readers, omniscient narrators make the text easier to understand because the narrator knows everything and reveals things as they become important. When the narrator changes or is unreliable, as is the case in *The Adventures of Huckleberry Finn* by Mark

Twain (1884) and *One Flew Over the Cuckoo's Nest* Ken Kesey (1962), the reader can be challenged.

Specifically for informational texts, there can be an authoritative narrator who has credibility based on experience or examples provided. In many cases, these narrators speak directly to the reader, as in "you will notice" or "when you assume too much," which serves to reengage the reader because the perspective is that the author is speaking directly to the reader. This format is not as common in narrative texts, but informational texts can successfully use the second-person point of view to reduce the text's difficulty level.

Graphic and Visual Information

Finally, the structure of the text can be analyzed in terms of how graphics and visual information, such as text features, are used. Different text features, such as bold words and charts, serve different purposes. A summary of some common text features and their functions is provided in Table 3.2. In some cases, the graphics used within the text demand

Table 3.2 Common Text Features in Secondary Textbooks

Type of Element	Text Features
Elements that organize	• Chapters • Titles • Headings • Subheadings • List of figures
Elements for locating information	• Table of contents • Indexes • Page numbers
Elements for explanation and elaboration	• Diagrams • Charts and tables • Graphs • Glossary
Elements that illustrate	• Photographs • Illustrations
Elements that notify	• Bolded words • Italics and other changes in font

Note. From *In a Reading State of Mind: Brain Research, Teacher Modeling, and Comprehension Instruction* (p. 102), by D. Fisher, N. Frey, and D. Lapp, 2009, Newark, DE: International Reading Association. Copyright 2009 by the International Reading Association.

attention and are required for understanding. In other cases, the graphic and visual information is used to create a more visually appealing page. When the graphics are necessary for understanding, the text is more complex. When the text features guide a reading, the text is less complex.

Language Conventionality and Clarity

In addition to the levels of meaning and the specific words that are used, some texts are more complex, and thus more difficult, because of the language conventionality and clarity. In part, this is due to the figurative language that is used. However, language conventionality and clarity are more than figurative language. As noted on the qualitative measures rubric, there are two additional factors that impact text complexity in this area: language variations and registers.

Standard English and Variations

When a reader reads a text that is consistent with his or her language usage, the text is easier. When the reader reads a text that contains variations from the language that the reader uses, the text is harder. Many of the books that students are expected to read are written in standard English. If students have experience with that form of language, then the texts are likely easier to understand. If they do not have a lot of experience with standard English, the texts will be more difficult. For example, *Gregor Mendel: The Friar Who Grew Peas* by Cheryl Bardoe (2006) was written in standard English and includes sentences such as these:

> Enterprising Gregor, by working as a tutor, paid his own way through four more years of school. Even when he was sick, Gregor never fell behind in his lessons. (p. 5)

Speakers of standard English will not likely find this book difficult to understand. English learners and students for whom standard English is less familiar might have more difficulty, and thus need more instruction, to make sense of the text.

Other books are written in different vernaculars or variations. These books are authentic in that they respect the time in which they are set or the language that is in use by the people profiled in the book. For example, reading a conversation between Jim and Huck in *The Adventures of Huckleberry Finn* requires an understanding of the language used at the time and place where the book is set. Consider Malik, a regular user of African American Vernacular English. When he read *The Watsons Go to Birmingham—1963* by Christopher Paul Curtis (1995), the text was not that complex for him. It fit Malik's experiences with language conventions. For example, this passage posed no problem for him:

> "I thought you was my friend. I didn't think you was like all them other people," he said. "I thought you was different." He didn't say this stuff like he was mad, he just sounded real, real sad. (p. 44)

But this text was very difficult for Amira, a student from Kenya who does not use African American Vernacular English. She is an English learner who has learned standard English, and the use of it in this text threw her off. Yet, the book was not so hard for Devin, a student who moved from rural Alabama to the city. The language conventionality was consistent with his experience growing up in the South.

Registers

In addition, there are a number of factors related to the formality of the language used in a text. Sociolinguists describe this phenomenon as language registers. Sociolinguists note that language registers are one of the ways in which social relationships reveal themselves in language.

> The concept of register is typically concerned with variations in language conditioned by uses rather than users and involves consideration of the situation or context of use, the purpose, subject matter, and content of the message, and the relationship between participants. (Romaine, 1994, p. 20)

The more registers a speaker possesses, the more able he or she is to communicate effectively in a variety of settings.

There are five generally agreed upon language registers (e.g., Joos, 1967; Payne, 1995):

1. *Fixed or frozen:* Fixed speech is reserved for traditions in which the language does not change. Examples of fixed speech include the Pledge of Allegiance, Shakespeare's plays, and civil ceremonies such as weddings.

2. *Formal:* At the formal level, speech is expected to be presented in complete sentences with specific word usage. Formal language is the standard for work, school, and business and is more often seen in writing than in speaking. However, public speeches and presentations are expected to be delivered in a formal language register.

3. *Consultative:* This third level of language is a formal register used in conversations and is less appropriate for writing. Students often use consultative language in their interactions in the classroom.

4. *Casual:* This is the language used in conversations with friends. In casual speech, word choice is general, and conversation is dependent upon nonverbal assists, significant background knowledge, and shared information.

5. *Intimate:* This language is used by very close friends and lovers. Intimate speech is private and often requires a significant amount of shared history, knowledge, and experience.

Payne (1995) argues that students often do not understand the match between the language register and the setting. She strongly advocates that teachers should provide students instruction in language registers. This requires teachers to scaffold students' use of language and not try to eliminate registers or dialects that students use in different settings. In other words, teaching students about language registers should be an additive model of education—one that encourages students to maintain their heritage language, dialect, and/or accent and provides them access to standard English (e.g., Brock, Boyd, & Moore, 2003; Townsend & Lapp, 2010).

Both of these factors, language variation and registers, influence the difficulty of the text. As with other qualitative dimensions, they are variables that deserve instructional attention, and like other qualitative dimensions, they are variables that teachers need to consider when they are working to ensure that students learn to read texts of sufficient complexity.

Knowledge Demands

Knowledge demand, like other quantitative and qualitative elements of text complexity, challenges readers because of the great variability in their backgrounds and experiences. These reader variables are considered in Chapter 4. When considering the suitability of a text segment, broader assumptions about knowledge demand can be located within the text. These include examining the level of prior knowledge needed to understand a text, as well as one's background knowledge and cultural knowledge. In addition, more formal vocabulary knowledge also plays an important role in knowledge demand.

Background Knowledge

The life experiences of a reader play a role in his or her understanding of a piece of text. This type of knowledge is typically gained informally and varies from one student to another. In regard to qualitative analysis of text, an examination of the content is in order. A simple story about nurturing a living plant or animal as it grows is likely to be a familiar experience for many young children. Conversely, the ability to recognize similar nurturing qualities of Mother Wolf as she raises Mowgli, a young boy, in *The Jungle Book* by Rudyard Kipling (1913) is likely to place more demand on the reader to move beyond his or her own direct experiences to project these qualities on a wolf who talks. The book's colonial India setting places some distance in both time and experience for young readers. Moreover, the book can be read and understood across multiple themes. Younger readers are likely to discern its themes of loyalty and friendship, whereas older students can look beyond these to the political commentary of British colonialism and the book's position as a moralistic text when it was first published.

Shifting perspectives can also challenge a reader. The picture book *Yo! Yes?* by Chris Raschka (1993) bounces the reader back and forth between two boys who carry on a conversation using nearly telegraphic speech. In 34 words, they express the hesitancy, fear of rejection, tentative offer, and finally celebration of a new friendship: "Yo! Yes? Hey? Who? You! Me?" (n.p.). This deceptively simple book requires quite a bit of background knowledge because the reader must shift between these two characters and attend to the spare dialogue, punctuation, font size, and illustrations to make sense of the story.

Older readers experience similar shifting perspectives in informational texts as well. *We Rode the Orphan Trains* by Andrea Warren (2001) moves frequently between third-person explanations of factual information to a first-person recollection. For instance, after two pages of a third-person account of a 4-year-old girl's experience of being chosen by an elderly man with a sick wife who wanted to adopt a child because "I need someone to wash the dishes" (p. 4), there is a shift to the recollection of the girl herself, many years later:

> When a couple standing nearby saw what was happening, the husband dashed to an ice-cream shop and returned with a strawberry cone.
>
> He knelt in front of me and asked, "Would you like to have this?" His voice was very gentle. "You can have one every day," he told me. An orphan never turns down food and I took the cone. I can still remember how good it tasted. I put my hand in his hand. He turned to his wife and said, "Minnie, let's take this little girl home." (p. 4)

The change in perspective is sudden, and the only clues a reader has are the extra space separating the first-person account from the third-person exposition, with its accompanying change in pronouns. There's no change in font, nor is it titled or set apart from the text as a boxed feature. These shifts in perspective can make an otherwise easier text more complex because the reader must attend to a change in the narration. Whether in literature or expository texts, a reader must draw on his or her life experiences about how information is conveyed between people and how it is recounted. Additionally, multiple themes can also increase a text's complexity.

Prior Knowledge

In addition to the life experiences that students gain, they also acquire more formal prior knowledge that must be used to understand new information in the text. In literary texts, this may be evidenced in a student's understanding of poetic form as he or she reads *Love That Dog* by Sharon Creech (2001). This sparse novel draws on several famous poems, notably "The Red Wheelbarrow" by William Carlos Williams and "Love That Boy" by Walter Dean Myers. The protagonist in the book mimics both the forms and the poetic language of these and other poems through journal entries. A story slowly unfolds as the boy reveals his own loss while ostensibly writing to his teacher about the assignments he is required to complete. This novel is deceptively simple, especially because the number of words per page never tops 100 and can be as few as eight.

Yet, this genre-bending book and the allusions to other texts make it more complex than any quantitative readability formula might measure.

Informational texts, particularly discipline-specific ones, can also be made more complex depending on the amount of formal academic knowledge needed to understand the reading. Consider, for instance, the amount of prior knowledge needed to understand Franklin Delano Roosevelt's "Pearl Harbor Address to the Nation" speech on December 8, 1941. After declaring that the previous date will "live in infamy," the president continues:

> The United States was at peace with that nation, and, at the solicitation of Japan, was still in conversation with its government and its emperor looking toward the maintenance of peace in the Pacific. Indeed, one hour after Japanese air squadrons had commenced bombing in the American island of Oahu, the Japanese ambassador to the United States and his colleague delivered to our secretary of state a formal reply to a recent American message. While this reply stated that it seemed useless to continue the existing diplomatic negotiations, it contained no threat or hint of war or armed attack. (para. 2)

Roosevelt's speech is a moment in time and presumes that his listeners understood his reference to "existing diplomatic negotiations" as well as the inference that the efforts toward "the maintenance of peace in the Pacific" included an embargo on trade that had continued in the months leading up to the attack. Knowledge demand is further intensified by references to the diplomatic mechanisms of the government and the role of the secretary of state. Add to this the required knowledge about Oahu's geographic location relative to U.S. mainland and an understanding of the genre of speeches, and you can begin to appreciate how this might challenge a high school student. The speech's fairly simple wording belies the complexity of the text itself.

Cultural Knowledge

Many texts allude to culturally bound references, and these can be the hardest to detect. As members of a culture, it can be quite difficult to distance oneself enough to be able to notice them (Ladson-Billings, 2006). For instance, Western literature primarily emanates from Judeo-Christian societies, and biblical references abound. Mention a prodigal son or a good Samaritan, and some students will understand that the reference is to a remorseful or selfless person. However, others will not. Some students come from other religious backgrounds or none at all. Others have little experience with how to interpret these references. Other cultural knowledge demands go beyond belief systems and can include the values, communication styles, and language proficiencies of a community (Ladson-Billings, 2006; Moll, Amanti, Neff, & Gonzalez, 1992).

Differences between students' experiences and those of the author of the text can contribute to a text's complexity. It is important to note that these cultural knowledge demands don't flow only in one direction. A student reading *Siddhartha* by Hermann Hesse (1922/1999) will be challenged by the novel's cultural knowledge demand about Buddhism, which makes this text comparatively more difficult than one situated in contemporary times, such as *It's Not About the Bike: My Journey Back to Life* by Lance Armstrong (2000). Although both are spiritual journeys of a sort, with wisdom won through suffering and sacrifice, the second book is likely to have less of a cultural knowledge demand than the first because of its well-known author, contemporary timeline, and sports setting. Those cultural knowledge differences that are situated with the learner are discussed in more detail in the next chapter.

Vocabulary Knowledge

Not to be overlooked is the vocabulary demand a text requires. These words and phrases serve as labels for ideas and concepts related to the knowledge demands of a piece. Analysis of vocabulary demand requires asking four questions:

1. Are there multiple-meaning words or phrases?
2. Do other elements of the text, especially text features, assist the reader?
3. Are there domain-specific labels that represent complex concepts?
4. Are there context clues that assist the reader in understanding these terms or phrases?

The domain-specific vocabulary used in the book *Guinea Pig Scientists: Bold Self-Experimenters in Science and Medicine* by Leslie Dendy and Mel Boring (2005) can be challenging:

In addition to the extermination of *Aedes aegypti* as a way to eliminate yellow fever, by 1937 there was a vaccination against the disease. Dr. Max Theiler helped develop the vaccine with the Rockefeller Foundation. It was called "17D" and is still used to protect people from yellow fever. (p. 83)

There is a heavy knowledge demand in these three sentences, with vocabulary serving as labels for complex ideas such as extermination (of an insect), elimination (of a disease), vaccination (to prevent contracting the disease), and even the mention of the source of funding (the Rockefeller Foundation). However, at least one text feature, the italicized Latin word, helps the reader understand that the authors are discussing the target of the disease. The reader may or may not have enough language or content knowledge regarding this or other diseases to know that it was an insect. However, the context clues (*protect people* contextualizes *vaccination*; *disease* contextualizes *yellow fever*) provide additional support for the reader.

Returning to *The Hunger Games*, Qualitatively

In Chapter 2, we used a passage from *The Hunger Games* (Collins, 2008) to highlight the various ways that readability formulas work. Recall that the readability of the book overall is at the 5.9 grade level, with content recommended for grades 7 and above. To consider the book qualitatively, we need to evaluate it using the factors previously identified. Recall that Figure 3.1 is a rubric that can be used to evaluate texts qualitatively.

Levels of Meaning and Purpose

The text focuses on a near distant future society, probably North America, that has experienced some event that has changed society from how we now know it. There is a literal story about children who are selected to fight one another, with the winner bringing glory to his or her state. There is a much deeper level of the text that relates to war, government control, reality television, poverty, and family bonds. The figurative language demands of the text are not extensive, but there are flashbacks and foreshadowing that readers must attend to if they are to fully grasp the text. There are also some concepts, especially those regarding the traditions and customs of this new world, that may confuse students.

Structure

The genre is likely familiar for students because dystopian novels are popular with adolescents and young adults (e.g., *The Giver* by Lois Lowry, The Uglies Trilogy by Scott Westerfeld, and *The Shadow Children* by Steven Schnur). *The Hunger Games* is told from a first-person narrator perspective. Naturally, the narrator is not omniscient, and thus events unfold for the reader as they do for the narrator. As we noted, there are a number of flashbacks that can confuse adolescent readers, but these are handled well and fairly clearly identified as such. The organization follows the story grammar structure that readers expect, and there are clear conflicts that are resolved.

Language Conventionality and Clarity

There are unfamiliar concepts in *The Hunger Games*, such as a mockingjay, but they are vividly described and explained. Overall, the language is conventional, with extensive dialogue used to forward the plot. Imagery and descriptions are used to describe the setting and events such that clarity is provided, yet the reader has to visualize a different world in the future. The narrator is conversational and appealing to young adults, both in terms of her actions and thoughts.

Knowledge Demands

The text places a fairly significant demand on a reader's knowledge base. Although readers will likely have a prior knowledge of the genre and some background knowledge about families and society, the text charts new ground in terms of a future world, the ways in which decisions are made, and how different states interact with one another within the nation. The major themes—facing a moral dilemma, government control over citizens, allegiances, war, and hunger—require readers' attention and reflection. There are many unique features of the world in which the main character, Katniss, lives. This is part of the appeal of the book and one of the reasons that it is difficult.

In reflecting on these qualitative aspects of the text, it seems reasonable to suggest that it is appropriate for middle school students. Having said that, there are many middle school students who do not have the background knowledge necessary to fully appreciate the themes that are developed within the text, which is probably why the book is also appealing to high school students and adults. In this case, the qualitative and quantitative analyses suggest a similar audience.

This is not always the case, such as with the book *By the Time You Read This, I'll Be Dead* by Julie Anne Peters (2010). Here's a representative passage from the book:

> Trash day. I keep a box of Glad bags behind the bottom drawer of my dresser. I hope Kim doesn't pull out the drawer. My clothes are sparse. I have underpants, socks, a bra. I've never owned much, since we move so often. I don't care about keeping stuff. I spread what little I have evenly between all four drawers. Behind the fourth drawer are my plastic bags. (p. 75)

The readability of this passage is at the 2.2 grade level, even though there are some much more complex terms, such as *Glad bags* and *sparse*. Other passages test at the 4.6 or 5.4 level. Yet, a closer look at the text, using the qualitative tools identified in this chapter, suggests that this is not appropriate for upper elementary or even middle school students. Later on the same page, the text reads, "Plastic bags are a suicide completer's best friend." The topics, voice, reasoning, and theme all place this book well above the readability. This is a perfect example of why qualitative measures are as important as quantitative ones.

Cautions and Criticisms of Qualitative Analysis of Text Complexity

Most discussions of quantitative measures of text complexity include a call for qualitative reviews of the text itself. As Hiebert (2011) notes, "Once quantitative data establish that particular texts are 'within the ballpark,' the hard work of qualitative analyzing the demands of texts in relation to different readers and tasks begins" (pp. 2–3). Having said that, there are some concerns about qualitative analyses, the first of which is the amount of time that teachers have available to complete these types of reviews. It is much faster to rely on readability formulas, but that does not provide the teacher with information about why and how a text is difficult. Understanding text difficulty is important because teachers can use that information in lesson planning. We are not suggesting that teachers should simply analyze texts and then avoid using hard ones with their students. Instead, we suggest that teachers should analyze texts to match students with texts and tasks and that teachers should plan instruction so students develop skills so they can read increasingly complex texts on their own (Mesmer, 2008).

Another caution of qualitative text complexity is based on the fact that validated tools are few and far between. Chall, Bissex, Conard, and Harris-Sharples (1996) used scaled text exemplars, criteria, and benchmarks to allow teachers to assess a piece of text qualitatively; however, they were unable to complete validation studies on their tool. In the absence of a validated tool, teachers should use indicators such as the rubric provided in Figure 3.1. Eventually, validated tools will be developed, and there will be new ways to think about qualitative text complexity. However, students cannot wait for those tools to be created.

Finally, because students and classrooms vary, the qualitative measures may reflect the expectations of teachers. What people think of as normal varies, based on experience and expertise. A teacher who has worked with affluent, high-performing students for 30 years may rate a text differently than a teacher who has effectively supported struggling readers over his or her career. We address this in greater detail in Chapter 4, but this is why qualitative measures are important. Students have different prior and background knowledge. This is also why the Common Core State Standards struck such a chord with so many people. In some places, the expectations placed on students were low, and students rose to those expectations. In other places, the expectations placed on students were high, and students rose to those expectations. Understanding how texts are complex will help us all teach and reach students based on high expectations rather than exist with the tyranny of low expectations.

Conclusion

Qualitative measures of text complexity can be used in conjunction with quantitative measures to determine the appropriateness of the text for the reader and the task. Of course, we have to also assess the reader and the task to make the match, which is the focus of Chapter 4. There has been a long history of analyzing texts qualitatively, with several decades' worth of work on understanding considerate texts. Yet, not all texts are considerate, and students need to learn to read increasingly complex and worthy texts. When teachers analyze texts for the levels of meaning or purpose, structure, language conventionality and clarity, and knowledge demands, they can plan appropriate instruction and guide learners' development.

REFERENCES

Alexander, P.A., Schallert, D.L., & Hare, V.C. (1991). Coming to terms: How researchers in learning and literacy talk about knowledge. *Review of Educational Research, 61*(3), 315–343.

Anderson, T.H., & Armbruster, B.B. (1984). Content area textbooks. In R.C. Anderson, J. Osborn, & R.J. Tierney (Eds.), *Learning to read in American schools: Basal readers and content texts* (pp. 193–224). Hillsdale, NJ: Erlbaum.

Armbruster, B.B. (1984). The problem of "inconsiderate text." In G.G. Duffy, L.R. Roehler, & J. Mason (Eds.), *Comprehension instruction: Perspectives and suggestions* (pp. 202–217). New York: Longman.

Armbruster, B.B. (1996). Considerate texts. In D. Lapp, J. Flood, & N. Farnan (Eds.), *Content area reading and learning: Instructional strategies* (2nd ed., pp. 47–58). Boston: Allyn & Bacon.

Bailin, A., & Grafstein, A. (2001). The linguistic assumptions underlying readability formulae: A critique. *Language & Communication, 21*(3), 285–301. doi:10.1016/S0271-5309(01)00005-2

Bakken, J.P., & Whedon, C.K. (2002). Teaching text structure to improve reading comprehension. *Intervention in School and Clinic, 37*(4), 229–233. doi:10.1177/105345120203700406

Baumann, J.F. (1986). Effect of rewritten content textbook passages on middle grade students' comprehension of main ideas: Making the inconsiderate considerate. *Journal of Reading Behavior, 18*(1), 1–21.

Boscolo, P., & Mason, L. (2003). Topic knowledge, text coherence, and interest: How they interact in learning from instructional texts. *The Journal of Experimental Education, 71*(2), 126–148. doi:10.1080/00220970309602060

Brock, C.H., Boyd, F.B., & Moore, J.A. (2003). Variation in language and the use of language across contexts: Implications for literacy learning. In J. Flood, D. Lapp, J.R. Squire, & J.M. Jensen (Eds.), *Handbook of research on teaching the English language arts* (2nd ed., pp. 446–458). Mahwah, NJ: Erlbaum.

Chall, J.S., Bissex, G.L., Conard, S.S., & Harris-Sharples, S. (1996). *Qualitative assessment of text difficulty: A practical guide for teachers and writers.* Cambridge, MA: Brookline.

Ciardiello, A.V. (2002). Helping adolescents understand cause/effect text structure in social studies. *The Social Studies, 93*(1), 31–36. doi:10.1080/00377990209599877

Dreher, M.J., & Singer, H. (1989). Friendly texts and text-friendly teachers. *Theory Into Practice, 28*(2), 98–104. doi:10.1080/00405848909543387

Duke, N.K. (2000). 3.6 minutes per day: The scarcity of informational texts in first grade. *Reading Research Quarterly, 35*(2), 202–224. doi:10.1598/RRQ.35.2.1

Fisher, D., & Frey, N. (2009). *Background knowledge: The missing piece of the comprehension puzzle.* Portsmouth, NH: Heinemann.

Fisher, D., & Frey, N. (2012). *Improving adolescent literacy: Content area strategies at work* (3rd ed.). Boston: Allyn & Bacon.

Fisher, D., Frey, N., & Lapp, D. (2009). *In a reading state of mind: Brain research, teacher modeling, and comprehension instruction.* Newark, DE: International Reading Association.

Fisher, D., Ross, D., & Grant, M. (2010). Building background knowledge. *The Science Teacher, 77*(1), 23–26.

Flood, J. (1986). The text, the student, and the teacher: Learning from exposition in middle schools. *The Reading Teacher, 39*(8), 784–791.

Flood, J., Mathison, C., Lapp, D., & Singer, H. (1989). Reading comprehension performance: The effects of teacher presentations and text features. *Reading Research and Instruction, 29*(1), 1–11. doi:10.1080/19388078909557991

Harvey, C.A., II. (2011). An inside view of Lexile measures: An interview with Malbert Smith III. *Knowledge Quest, 39*(4), 56–59.

Hiebert, E.H. (2011). *Using multiple sources of information in establishing text complexity* (Reading Research Report No. 11.03). Santa Cruz, CA: TextProject & University of California, Santa Cruz. Retrieved January 4, 2012, from textproject. org/research/reading-research-reports/a-case-for-using-multiple-sources-of-information-in-establishing-text-complexity/

Joos, M. (1967). *The five clocks.* New York: Harcourt, Brace & World.

Kobayashi, M. (2002). Method effects on reading comprehension test performance: Text organization and response format. *Language Testing, 19*(2), 193–220. doi:10.1191/0265532202lt227oa

Konopak, B.C. (1988). Effects of inconsiderate vs. considerate text on secondary students' vocabulary learning. *Journal of Reading Behavior, 20*(1), 25–41.

Ladson-Billings, G. (2006). Yes, but how do we do it? Practicing culturally relevant pedagogy. In J. Landsman & C.W. Lewis (Eds.), *White teachers/diverse classrooms: A guide to building inclusive schools, promoting high expectations, and eliminating racism* (pp. 29–42). Sterling, VA: Stylus.

Lapp, D., & Flood, J. (1982). Teaching a text. In H. Singer (Ed.), *Proceedings of the Learning From Text Committee* (pp. 82–86). Sacramento: California Department of Education.

Lively, B.A., & Pressey, S.L. (1923). A method for measuring the 'vocabulary burden' of textbooks. *Educational Administration and Supervision, 9,* 389–398.

McCabe, A., & Rollins, P.R. (1994). Assessment of preschool narrative skills. *American Journal of Speech-Language Pathology, 3,* 45–56.

McNamara, D.S., & Kintsch, W. (1996). Learning from texts: Effects of prior knowledge and text coherence. *Discourse Processes, 22*(3), 247–288. doi:10.1080/01638539609544975

Mesmer, H.A.E. (2008). *Tools for matching readers to texts: Research-based practices.* New York: Guilford.

Meyer, B.J.F. (2003). Text coherence and readability. *Topics in Language Disorders, 23*(3), 204–224. doi:10.1097/00011363-200307000-00007

Moll, L.C., Amanti, C., Neff, D., & Gonzalez, N. (1992). Funds of knowledge for teaching: Using a qualitative approach to connect homes and classrooms. *Theory Into Practice, 31*(2), 132–141. doi:10.1080/00405849209543534

National Governors Association Center for Best Practices & Council of Chief State School Officers. (2010). *Common Core State Standards for English language arts and literacy in history/social studies, science, and technical subjects: Appendix A: Research supporting key elements of the standards and glossary of key terms.* Washington, DC: Authors.

Parsons, J. (2000). Helping students learn how textbooks are written. *Canadian Social Studies, 35*(1). Retrieved January 4, 2012, from www2.education.ualberta.ca/css/css_35_1/classroom_tips.htm#Classroom Tips

Payne, R.K. (1995). *A framework for understanding and working with students and adults from poverty.* Baytown, TX: RFT.

Romaine, S. (1994). *Language in society: An introduction to sociolinguistics.* New York: Oxford University Press.

Sanders, T. (1997). Semantic and pragmatic sources of coherence: On the categorization of coherence relations in context. *Discourse Processes, 24*(1), 119–147. doi:10.1080/01638539709545009

Seda, M.M., Ligouri, O.Z., & Seda, C.M. (1999). Bridging literacy and social studies: Engaging prior knowledge through children's books. *TESOL Journal, 8*(3), 34–40.

Shanahan, T., & Shanahan, C. (2008). Teaching disciplinary literacy to adolescents: Rethinking content-area literacy. *Harvard Educational Review, 78*(1), 40–59.

Townsend, D.R., & Lapp, D. (2010). Academic language, discourse communities, and technology: Building students' linguistic resources. *Teacher Education Quarterly.* Retrieved January 4, 2012, from teqjournal.org/townsend_lapp.html

LITERATURE CITED

Ali, N. (with Minoui, D.). (2010). *I am Nujood, age 10 and divorced* (L. Cloverdale, Trans.). New York: Three Rivers.

Armstrong, L. (with S. Jenkins). (2000). *It's not about the bike: My journey back to life.* New York: G.P. Putnam's Sons.

Bardoe, C. (2006). *Gregor Mendel: The friar who grew peas.* New York: Harry N. Abrams.

Beeler, S.B. (1998). *Throw your tooth on the roof: Tooth traditions from around the world.* Boston: Houghton Mifflin.

Bogacki, T. (1996). *Cat and mouse.* New York: Farrar Straus & Giroux.

Browne, A. (1998). *Voices in the park.* New York: DK.

Chekhov, A. (1999). An upheaval. In *Anton Chekhov: Early short stories, 1883–1888* (S. Foote, Ed., & C. Garnett, Trans.; pp. 131–138). New York: Random House.

Collins, S. (2008). *The hunger games.* New York: Scholastic.

Creech, S. (2001). *Love that dog.* New York: HarperCollins.

Curtis, C.P. (1995). *The Watsons go to Birmingham—1963.* New York: Bantam Doubleday Dell.

Dendy, L., & Boring, M. (2005). *Guinea pig scientists: Bold self-experimenters in science and medicine.* New York: Henry Holt.

Hesse, H. (1999). *Siddhartha* (S. Appelbaum, Trans.). Mineola, NY: Dover. (Original work published 1922)

Innocenti, R. (1985). *Rose Blanche.* Mankato, MN: Creative Editions.

Kafka, F. (1946). *Metamorphosis* (A.L. Lloyd, Trans.). New York: Vanguard.

Kesey, K. (1962). *One flew over the cuckoo's nest.* New York: Viking.

Kipling, R. (1913). *The jungle book*. New York: Century.

Marschall, K., & Brewster, H. (1997). *Inside the Titanic*. Boston: Madison.

Mikaelsen, B. (1998). *Petey*. New York: Hyperion.

Orwell, G. (1946). *Animal farm*. New York: Harcourt, Brace.

Peters, J.A. (2010). *By the time you read this, I'll be dead*. New York: Hyperion.

Raschka, C. (1993). *Yo! Yes?* New York: Orchard.

Roosevelt, F.D. (Speaker). (1941). *"A date which will live in infamy": FDR asks for a declaration of war*. Retrieved January 5, 2012, from historymatters.gmu.edu/d/5166

Seuss, Dr. (pseud. T.S. Geisel). (1957). *How the Grinch stole Christmas*. New York: Random House.

Seuss, Dr. (pseud. T.S. Geisel). (1958). Yertle the turtle. In *Yertle the turtle, and other stories* (pp. 1–30). New York: Random House.

Seuss, Dr. (pseud. T.S. Geisel). (1961). The Sneetches. In *The Sneetches, and other stories* (pp. 1–25). New York: Random House.

Seuss, Dr. (pseud. T.S. Geisel). (1971). *The Lorax*. New York: Random House.

Shakespeare, W. (2009). *As you like it* (Rev. ed.; M. Hattaway, Ed.). New York: Cambridge University Press.

Sloan, C. (2002). *Bury the dead: Tombs, corpses, mummies, skeletons, and rituals*. Washington, DC: National Geographic.

Taback, S. (1997). *There was an old lady who swallowed a fly*. New York: Viking.

Twain, M. (1884). *The adventures of Huckleberry Finn*. London: Chatto & Windus.

Warren, A. (2001). *We rode the orphan trains*. Boston: Houghton Mifflin.

Weber, B. (2004). *Animal disguises*. Boston: Kingfisher.

CHAPTER 4

Matching Readers to Texts and Tasks

While the prior two elements of the model focus on the inherent complexity of text, variables specific to particular readers (such as motivation, knowledge, and experiences) and to particular tasks (such as purpose and the complexity of the task assigned and the questions posed) must also be considered when determining whether a text is appropriate for a given student. Such assessments are best made by teachers employing their professional judgment, experience, and knowledge of their students and the subject.

—NGA & CCSSO, 2010b, p. 4

The writer of a text always presumes a reader's knowledge. A reference guide written for pharmacists, such as *Drug Interactions Analysis and Management 2011* by Philip Hansten and John Horn (2011), presumes a high degree of prior knowledge on the part of its reader. Conversely, *The Pill Book* by Harold Silverman (2010), with its photographs, extensive glossary, and subheadings (e.g., "Prescribed For," "Cautions and Warnings," "Possible Side Effects"), is specifically written for the layperson, one who does not possess advanced training in the subject. Judging by their longevity (the first is in its sixth edition, the second in its 14th), both do their jobs exceedingly well. Yet, a pharmacist would be frustrated by the lack of technical information in *The Pill Book*, whereas the worried parent of a 4-year-old breaking out in a strange rash after switching to a new cough syrup would be confused by the information in *Drug Interactions Analysis and Management 2011*. Neither book is better or worse than the other; they vary in the amount of knowledge required to understand them. As such, they are appropriate for different audiences.

The third aspect of text complexity identified in the Common Core State Standards (NGA & CCSSO, 2010b) acknowledges this issue:

> Harder texts may be appropriate for highly knowledgeable or skilled readers, and easier texts may be suitable as an expedient for building struggling readers' knowledge or reading skill up to the level required by the Standards. Highly motivated readers are often willing to put in the extra effort required to read harder texts that tell a story or contain information in which they are deeply interested. Complex tasks may require the kind of information contained only in similarly complex texts. (p. 7)

This is not to say that struggling readers only read easier texts or that skilled readers only read hard texts. Readers read for a variety of purposes, and all of us like to read texts that are comfortable for us, especially when we are looking for new information. For example, when Doug was asked to develop a new online class and not simply use discussion boards and postings, he searched for some reading material that would help him with this task. *The Exceptional Presenter Goes Virtual: Take Command of Your Message, Create an "In-Person" Experience and Captivate Any Remote Audience* by Timothy Koegel (2010) provided Doug with information that he could use and that he understood.

In terms of matching the reader and the task, Doug had the cognitive capability to read the selected text independently, he was motivated to learn more about the topic because of a task that he needed to complete, and his background knowledge included presenting, but not presenting in a virtual environment. Understanding these factors requires an exploration of the reader.

In addition, Doug was reading independently, so the text needed to contain enough scaffolds for him to successfully work his way through the information. Had he been working in a group, the selected text could have been more difficult. Alternatively, he could have taken a class and worked with a teacher using a much more difficult text. Understanding these factors requires an exploration of the task required of the reader.

Finally, when asked by the instructional technology designer about what he wanted to do with the information and how he would build his virtual classroom, Doug had to know how to respond to these questions. Like other skilled readers, he returned to the text often to locate information and justify his responses. Understanding these factors requires an exploration of the questions used to guide readers' thinking and use of evidence. Each of these explorations—the reader, the task, and the question—is the focus of this chapter. A checklist for analyzing texts for their match with readers and tasks is provided in Figure 4.1.

Figure 4.1 Checklist for Matching Readers to Texts

Exploring the Reader	Notes
Cognitive Capabilities	
Will this text maintain the student's attention?	
Will this text tax the reader's working memory?	
Will this text require specialized supports (e.g., language support, accommodations)?	
Does this text contain enough supports to move the reader's learning forward rather than cause frustration?	
Motivation	
Does the topic or genre of the text interest the reader?	
Is the text relevant to the reader?	
Does the reader have an opportunity to exercise choice?	
Has the reader experienced success in the past with this topic or genre?	
Does the reader have opportunities to collaborate with others before and after the reading?	
Is the text being used to connect to larger themes or concepts?	
Will this text allow the reader to meet a goal that he or she has set?	
Knowledge	
Does the reader possess specialized knowledge about the topic or genre?	
Does the reader possess the needed metacognitive skills to comprehend the text?	
Does the reader have sufficient background and/ or prior knowledge to link to new information?	

(continued)

Figure 4.1 Checklist for Matching Readers to Texts (continued)

Experiences	
What direct experiences does the reader have that may make this text more accessible?	
Is this text more complex than previous ones to build the reader's skills and knowledge?	
Exploring the Task	
Teacher-Led Tasks	
Does this text require modeling of cognitive comprehension strategies?	
Does this text require modeling of word-solving strategies?	
Does this text require modeling of text structures?	
Does this text require modeling of text features?	
Peer Tasks	
Does the task match the reader's' collaborative learning skills?	
Does the task match the readers' social skills?	
Does the task require the readers to engage in accountable talk?	
Are suitable supports for accountable talk (e.g., language frames) furnished?	
Individual Tasks	
Does the task provide sufficient challenge for the reader while avoiding protracted frustration?	
Are the text and the task sufficiently more complex than previous ones so they provide opportunities to build the reader's skills and knowledge?	
Exploring the Question	
Do the questions require the reader to return to the text?	
Do the questions require the reader to use evidence to support his or her ideas or claims?	
Do the questions move from text-explicit to text-implicit knowledge?	
Are there questions that require the reader to analyze, evaluate, and create?	

Exploring the Reader

The previous chapters focused on the text because deeply examining a reading is essential for determining instruction. However, the most important factor, the reader, is what makes a text come to life. Until a reader explores the pages of a book, it is simply a collection of words. As Rosenblatt (2003) notes, a reader's transaction with the text becomes the place where meaning is created:

> In the efferent reading, attention is focused predominantly on abstracting out, analyzing, and structuring what is to be retained after the reading, e.g., factual information or analysis. In an aesthetic reading, attention is focused predominantly on what is being lived through during the reading, the ideas and feelings being evoked and organized as the work corresponding to the text. This evocation constitutes the work that is the object of interpretation and evaluation. (p. 70)

When reading any passage, a student builds meaning in collaboration with the author. Until that occurs, an assessment of a text's complexity is not yet fully realized. The reader is a key ingredient in this formula.

Rosenblatt's seminal work in literary criticism beginning in the 1930s has had a profound and far-reaching influence on the field of reading instruction. Other researchers have collectively deepened our understanding of how we position the reader as the linchpin. The RAND Reading Study Group (2002), synthesizing this research, identified many such factors:

> The reader brings to the act of reading his or her cognitive capabilities (attention, memory, critical analytic ability, inferencing, visualization); motivation (a purpose for reading, interest in the content, self-efficacy as a reader); knowledge (vocabulary and topic knowledge, linguistic and discourse knowledge, knowledge of comprehension strategies); and experiences. (pp. xiii–xiv)

We discuss each of these factors in further detail to explore the dimensions of understanding that a reader brings to the text to support comprehension.

Cognitive Capabilities

Whereas the passage from the RAND report locates cognitive capabilities within the reader, we take a broader view of this concept to include our capability as teachers to utilize and extend these factors. Given that reading is not a fixed ability, but rather something that is learned, understanding who the reader is makes us capable to choose the right text for the right student and pair it with the right instruction.

To be sure, attention and memory are key variables in reading for meaning. Visual attention to print is essential in the development of reading but not a given among emergent readers. Studies of young children engaged in storybook reading have found that they attend to print 3–7% of the time, spending most of it looking at the pictures. However, when the adult prompted the children's attention through verbal inquiries and gestures, the time the children spent attending to the print increased significantly (Justice, Pullen, & Pence, 2008). Asking them, "Can you show me the letter *b* in this word?," pointing to the speech bubble on a page with dialogue, or tracking the print with a finger while reading nearly doubled the amount of time they spent attending to print. Interesting, the researchers also found that the nonverbal interactions resulted in more fixations on print than the verbal ones did. The authors further projected that for a child who is read to for 10 minutes a day, this would result in 18,000 more fixations on print in the course of one year.

The growing ability of a reader to attend to text is directly related to one's working memory capacity (sometimes incorrectly called short-term memory). All readers need to temporarily store letters and words to manipulate them so they can be decoded, and meaning can be assigned (Kintsch & Van Dijk, 1978). Attention and working memory are executive functions, meaning that the reader is able to influence them to some degree. However, background knowledge, prior experiences, and vocabulary knowledge are also factors, perhaps explaining up to 66% of the variance between readers with strong comprehension skills and those who struggle to understand (Cromley & Azevedo, 2007). Working memory for reading comprehension is further strengthened by conscious choice to limit intrusive thoughts (i.e., mind wandering) so the reader can maintain focus on the passage (McVay & Kane, 2011). In the same way that our instructional practices can positively influence young students' attention to print, we can similarly direct the attention of older readers by clearly establishing purpose for them before they read (Fisher & Frey, 2011b).

There are, of course, variations among children. Students who are learning English must divide their attention and working memory to make meaning (Thomas, Healy, & Greenberg, 2007). Some readers have identified language or learning differences that require us to provide more specialized supports. Others have fewer formal language experiences than their classmates. However, variances among the students in our classrooms cannot result in lowered expectations for their learning, especially by systematically denying them access to the kinds of rich text experiences of others (e.g., Taylor, 1990). Instead, we must find ways to scaffold their reading experiences by differentiating instruction and providing accommodations and modifications as warranted (e.g., Roller, 1996). These are teaching concepts that we have known for decades, and the introduction of the Common Core State Standards should not be viewed as a retreat from these practices.

Motivation

A student who is motivated to read something can far exceed our expectations of what he or she should be capable of reading. We have witnessed adolescents labeled as struggling readers who pore over technical manuals and blogs discussing the operation of a piece of technology that they're interested in reading about. Many of us have known a younger child who can seemingly digest an informational book about a topic of acute interest to him or her—poisonous spiders, horses, or space exploration— and discuss these in detail with others. A motivated reader is one who engages in significantly more reading than one who is not motivated to do so. Wigfield and Guthrie (1997) have identified a 300% difference in time spent reading between intrinsically motivated and unmotivated fourth- and fifth-grade readers. Although we don't expect young students to identify their college and career plans, we notice these sparks of interest among our students and place interesting (and yes, complex) texts in their paths. When we do so, students engage with texts for hours.

However, our concern is that the concept of intrinsic motivation gets confounded with internal characteristics of the actual reader. We assert that intrinsic motivation in students is largely influenced by situational conditions and that even highly motivated readers can find their enthusiasm dampened because of circumstances. Nancy recalls a time when she briefly joined an adult book club (something she was highly motivated to do) only to quickly discover that one person in the group controlled all the conversations, interrupted others, and cut people off when they disagreed with her. In short order, Nancy became a book club dropout, even though her interest in the book itself remained high. In large part, instructional practices can contribute to, or detract from, a student's motivation to read. In their review of the role of motivation in reading, McRae and Guthrie (2009) have identified five teaching practices that foster motivation, and five that destroy it. The following instructional practices impact motivation positively:

1. Relevance
2. Choice
3. Success
4. Collaboration
5. Thematic units

Avoid these five practices because they have a negative effect:

1. Nonrelevance
2. Excessive control
3. Difficult lessons
4. Frequent individual work
5. Disconnected units

To distill these further, we group across two dimensions, both of which teachers strongly influence: curricular organization and social interactions. Organization of the curriculum is largely responsible for the degree to which we can ground relevance by establishing purpose in lessons, in the ways we design units to promote further investigation of a topic, and in how we foster choice within those investigations (Fisher, Frey, & Lapp, 2012). In addition, instruction should be aligned with the principles of social interaction as a necessary condition of learning. To propel learning forward, we need students to engage in incrementally more demanding (but not impossible) tasks—in the company of others who are learning and with expert guidance close at hand when the group gets stuck.

We add one more dimension to this list: goal setting. It is important to note that motivation is not limited to interest or enjoyment of the task itself. We think of the athlete who spends many hours in isolation, hitting baseballs or shooting free throws. The motivation in these cases is not because the task is so enjoyable but rather that the athlete recognizes that putting in the hours of practice will result in improved performance. Ericsson, Krampe, and Tesch-Römer (1993) call this deliberate practice the "repeated experiences in which the individual can attend to the critical aspects of the situation and incrementally improve her or his performance in response to knowledge of results, feedback, or both from a teacher" (p. 368). Teachers can promote deliberate practice through goal setting with students when they link goal-setting activities back to the established purposes. In other words, goal setting should be a regular part of the instructional design process.

Knowledge

We return to the knowledge demand factors first discussed in Chapter 3 to examine them in more detail from the viewpoint of the learner. As noted earlier in this book, all texts place a certain amount of knowledge demand on a reader, if for no other reason than the fact that even the simplest text couldn't fully explain every detail. ("Old MacDonald had a farm. Old MacDonald is the name of the farmer. A farmer raises animals and crops. Crops are edible plants grown on large plots of land...." You get the idea.)

Yet, possession of requisite knowledge is insufficient. Learners must also be practiced at accessing that information. Here is where novices to any skill or concept falter—they are not especially good at using needed information to understand newer knowledge. The competition for attention is just too great. In an effort to attend to new information, they temporarily forget about other cognitive resources that they otherwise know. In other words, it's not so much a question of whether they possess the necessary prior knowledge and background experiences but whether they are able to marshal these resources when needed.

Accessing known knowledge requires the reader to be able to engage in metacognitive thinking. Thinking about one's thinking is essential for pairing the known with the unknown (Donovan & Bransford, 2005) and is a critical factor in distinguishing a novice from an expert (Ericsson & Charness, 1994). A dimension of metacognition is self-management, explained by Cross and Paris (1988) as consisting of the following:

> three categories: evaluation, planning, and regulation. In the context of reading, evaluation refers to analyses of task characteristics and personal

abilities that affect comprehension. Planning involves the selection of particular strategies to reach the goals that have been set or chosen. Regulation is the monitoring and redirection of one's activities during the course of reading to reach the desired goals. (p. 131)

Further, their work with third- and fifth-grade readers found that instruction about metacognitive thinking led to increased comprehension and performance, most notably among students who were identified as reading below grade level. As with other factors about the reader, metacognitive knowledge is not innate and static, but rather it can be directly influenced through purposeful instruction. We discuss these methods in more detail in the next chapter.

Experiences

Of all the factors we have discussed regarding the reader, his or her experiences may appear to be the most far removed from our influence. It is true that you cannot rewind the clock to make sure that students were exposed to rich interactive language when they were babies or that they were regularly read to as toddlers. However, we can capitalize on their current experiences. For example, field trips and other out-of-class excursions are a regular feature of school but are not always used as fruitfully as they could be in reading development. To do so, students should be reading related texts in advance of a field trip to build topical knowledge and also afterward to deepen and extend their understanding. A kindergarten trip to the local zoo should include shared readings of books like'Twas the Day Before Zoo Day by Catherine Ipcizade (2008) or I Want to Be a Zookeeper by Daniel Liebman (2003) before students travel there. After this experience, students are ready for more complex texts, such as Zoo by Gail Gibbons (1991) and Aliki's (1997) My Visit to the Zoo. In this way, both texts and experiences are coordinated to scaffold students' understanding of more complex texts.

Exploring the Task

In addition to understanding the reader, it is important to consider how the reader will use the text. In selecting texts for classroom use, teachers need to consider more than the quantitative and qualitative scores given to the reading. What students are expected to do with the text impacts the types of texts that are appropriate. Simply said, when students are asked to read independently, the selected texts have to be reasonably matched to their performance level. If teachers want students to access more complex texts, teachers have to teach the texts. This is what the Common Core State Standards are about: increasing the rigor of what students can read through high-quality instruction. The standards do not say to make students read things that are too hard for them by themselves. The standards suggest that students should encounter texts that are complex, learn to notice what is confusing, and then receive instruction in those areas of confusion. In other words, to effectively implement the Common Core State Standards, or any other effort to increase rigor and complexity, the teacher has to share in the responsibility and do some of the work.

Teacher-Led Tasks

When the teacher is leading the task, the selected texts can be much more complex. Teacher-led tasks are typically those in which the teacher is modeling his or her thinking. As apprentices, students need to have thinking made visible. Thinking is invisible, and the only way to illuminate it for students is to talk about it. As Duffy (2003) notes,

> The only way to model thinking is to talk about how to do it. That is, we provide a verbal description of the thinking one does or, more accurately, an *approximation* of the thinking involved (since there is no one way to do any reading task). (p. 11)

In the area of reading, there are a number of components that teachers can model, including comprehension, word solving, text structures, and text features. Table 4.1 contains a summary as well as a definition for each of these components.

In terms of comprehension, teachers can model the use of cognitive strategies such as visualizing, inferring, summarizing, predicting, questioning, or monitoring. These cognitive strategies should be used when appropriate based on clues from the text. They should not be curricularized, with four weeks devoted to summarizing, for example, and then the next four weeks devoted to predicting. Readers have to learn to notice the text clues that trigger specific, useful cognitive strategies. As we noted in Chapter 1, this is consistent with the behavior of skilled

Table 4.1 Dimensions of Interactive Comprehension Modeling

Dimension	Definition	Components
Vocabulary	Focus on solving an unknown word, not providing the definition of the word	• Context clues • Word parts (prefix, suffix, root, base, related words) • Use of resources (peers, dictionary, Internet)
Comprehension	Strategic moves to support understanding the text	• Summarizing/synthesize • Predicting • Inferring • Visualizing • Questioning • Connecting • Monitoring • Activating background knowledge
Text structures	Structures used in presenting information that readers can use to predict the flow of information	• Cause/effect • Compare/contrast • Problem/solution • Temporal/sequence • Descriptive • Story grammar (plot, setting, character, conflict, etc.)
Text features	Components of the text added to increase understanding or interest	• Captions • Illustrations, diagrams • Headings, titles • Bold, italic words • Glossary, index

Note. Reprinted from "'You Can Read This Text—I'll Show You How': Interactive Comprehension Instruction," by D. Lapp, D. Fisher, and M. Grant, 2008, *Journal of Adolescent & Adult Literacy, 51*(5), p. 381. Copyright 2008 by the International Reading Association.

readers who have reached automaticity with cognitive strategies and mobilize them when appropriate. Just as important, students need to see that these are ultimately problem-solving approaches to be used when meaning breaks down. Getting good at using problem-solving strategies requires students to have opportunities to do so. In other words, they need exposure to texts in the hands of someone who can show them how a problem is resolved.

In addition to cognitive strategies, teachers can model their word solving of vocabulary by noticing word parts (morphology), context clues, or the use of resources. During modeling, the point is not to teach individual words or simply tell students what words mean but rather to develop students' habits in word solving. Parenthetically, this point is consistent with one of the Common Core State Standards, namely anchor standard number 4 for language: "Determine or clarify the meaning of unknown and multiple-meaning words and phrases by using context clues, analyzing meaningful word parts, and consulting general and specialized reference materials, as appropriate" (NGA & CCSSO, 2010a, p. 25). When teachers model these behaviors, students begin to develop a habit and use word solving when they encounter unknown or unfamiliar words. As students do so, they can independently read increasingly complex texts.

Further, teachers can model their use of text structures to understand the text and predict what the author will proffer next. For example, when the author provides a cause for something such as the Great Depression, the reader should expect an effect. Similarly, when the author introduces a problem, the reader understands that a solution is likely forthcoming. In terms of narrative texts, teachers can model how literary devices help them understand the text. For example, while reading *Click, Clack, Moo: Cows That Type* by Doreen Cronin (2000) with first graders, the teacher first noted that structure helped her understand that the book was nonfiction:

> "I'm seeing on this first page that the cows are typing. I know that cows don't really type, so I think that this is probably fiction. I know that authors sometimes use animals that talk to make a point and teach me something. I'll read on and see what that is."

In addition to literary devices, teachers can model their understanding of story grammar. As we discussed in the previous chapter, most narrative texts follow a consistent structure. Later, after reading more of *Click, Clack, Moo*, the teacher said,

> "I think that this is our conflict. I remember that the cows wrote a letter to the farmer asking for electric blankets because the barn was closed. Now, they are on strike, and the sign says, 'No milk today.' I expect that the farmer will be very unhappy, and this conflict will have to be resolved."

Again, this is consistent with the Common Core State Standards, as noted in anchor standard 5 for reading: "Analyze the structure of texts, including how specific sentences, paragraphs, and larger portions of the text (e.g., a section, chapter, scene, or stanza) relate to each other and the whole" (NGA & CCSSO, 2010a, p. 35).

Finally, teachers can model their use of text features. We discussed the various types of text features in Chapter 3 but did not comment on the ways in which students can learn to use the text features on their own. When teachers model their use of these features, students learn to apply the approach to new and more complex texts. For example, in the second-grade reading standard of the Common Core State Standards for informational text, students are expected to "know and use various text features (e.g., captions, bold print, subheadings, glossaries, indexes, electronic menus, icons) to locate key facts or information in a text efficiently" (p. 13). Students can probably do this already, but they may not do so in complex texts. When the teacher models with difficult texts, students begin to see how to apply what they have learned in new ways.

Importantly, modeling should include metacognitive discussions related to how the teacher thought about the text, not just which strategies the teacher used while reading. For example, while reading *From the Mixed-Up Files of Mrs. Basil E. Frankweiler* by E.L. Konigsburg (1967), fourth-grade teacher Ms. Cruise stopped after reading a section about looking for fingerprints on a statue that might have been made by Michelangelo. The text reads,

> Jamie snapped his fingers. "I've got it!" he exclaimed. He held up his hands for Claudia to see.
> "What does that mean?"
> "Fingerprints, silly. If Michelangelo worked on that statue, his fingerprints would be on it." (pp. 62–63)

Ms. Cruise provided modeling for the students:

> "I was trying to visualize this in my mind. I can see Michelangelo working on the statue and getting his fingerprints all over it, but I'm thinking about something else. If Michelangelo made the statue, it would be really old because he lived in the 1500s. And I wonder if the fingerprints would still be on the statue after all of those years. I also wonder if anyone saved Michelangelo's fingerprints. If there were fingerprints on the statue, and no one had Michelangelo's fingerprints, then this wouldn't work. I think that there are too many complications for this to work to prove the statue was created by Michelangelo. I predict that they are going to have to find another way to figure this out. I keep thinking about the title of the book and wondering if there is better information about the statue in those mixed-up files because we haven't heard much about the files yet, and the author did put that in the title."

Table 4.2 offers a sample of teacher modeling with older students that focuses on informational text. Maria, the teacher profiled in the figure, asked her students to read the text first and notice what was confusing. In many situations, it is appropriate for students to meet a complex text first,

Table 4.2 Sample Teacher Modeling

Text	Teacher Commentary During the Think-Aloud	Strategies Modeled/Practiced
Going Through Changes (Photo of pancakes)	"As I look over this piece of text, I see a photo of pancakes cooking on a griddle. Some are golden brown and others are still a beige batter color. The title of this reading is Going Through Changes. I wonder if the pancakes, some uncooked and others fully done, represent changes at a chemical level. I'll read the first paragraph."	Predicting and using titles and graphics provides focus and motivation to read further.
At a dinner table, a cook is making pancakes. He mixes together an egg, milk, and flour into a batter. When the batter is placed on the griddle, it becomes solid and golden brown. The batter has had a chemical change. All the atoms of the original ingredients are still in the batter. But the griddle's heat has arranged those atoms in a different pattern. Like the pancake batter, many substances go through chemical changes. These changes can break down complex substances into simpler parts. Or they can join simple parts into complex substances.	"So the cooking batter does represent chemical changes. I see from reading these paragraphs that chemical changes involve substances breaking down and substances joining together. I think the next section will tell me about how this process of breaking down and building up occurs. Do you have any ideas?" (Maria listens as the students share a few possibilities.) Janette, a student in Maria's class, responds, "Maybe the next section will talk about molecules being broken down or atoms being joined together." Dave adds, "Yes, I remember when I was in 8th grade we talked about how salt molecules are broken down when salt is added to water." Maria then continues. "OK, let's read on to see if we're correct."	The prediction is confirmed by reading the text. Note that sometimes the prediction is refuted after reading the text. Afterward, the main ideas are identified by summarizing a few lines of the text, which is followed by another prediction based on the text just read.

(continued)

Table 4.2 Sample Teacher Modeling (continued)

Text	Teacher Commentary During the Think-Aloud	Strategies Modeled/ Practiced
It usually takes energy to combine substances in a chemical reaction. This kind of reaction is called an endothermic reaction.	"An endothermic reaction. Wow, I'm not sure what that means, but I do know that thermic sounds like a word part from thermometer or thermal and both of those terms relate to heat. Maybe endothermic also relates to heat in some way. I'll continue to read. Maybe I'll gain an understanding of the meaning of this word if I read on."	Segmenting words into word parts brings attention to root words or affixes that might offer clues to meaning. In addition, understanding that clarification might come from context or from continued reading.
For example, heat was needed to turn the batter into a pancake.	"I guess I was right—endothermic does relate to heat."	Again, confirmation of a prediction, in this case of a word's meaning, may be confirmed or refuted by reading upcoming text.
If iron and powdered sulfur were mixed together, nothing would happen. But apply heat to those combined substances and you would form iron sulfide. This is an entirely new substance.	"So heat added to a mixture can cause a new substance to form. Interesting. Maybe endothermic means that heat is added."	Synthesizes and restates—examples offered in the text can help the reader to infer word meaning.

Note. Quotes from TIME and Teacher Created Materials (1993). Reprinted from "'You Can Read This Text—I'll Show You How': Interactive Comprehension Instruction," by D. Lapp, D. Fisher, and M. Grant, 2008, *Journal of Adolescent & Adult Literacy, 51*(5), pp. 373–374. Copyright 2008 by the International Reading Association.

identify what caused them difficulty, and then hear their teacher's thinking about the text. At other times, as was the case in Ms. Cruise's classroom, teacher modeling occurs as the students see the text for the first time. These instructional decisions are made, in part, based on the demand of the text and the skills of the students.

Peer Tasks

When students are invited to collaborate, the texts can be complex but perhaps not as complex as the texts that teachers use in modeling. Having said that, the texts used during group work should also not be so easy as to remove any challenge or struggle from the experience. As we discussed in Chapter 1, struggle is important to learning, and this is especially true in group work when students have peer support and interaction to guide their understanding. Peer tasks provide students with time to work together to clarify their understanding of skills and concepts that they are learning. To do so, students must have a task that is sufficiently complex enough that errors can occur (Frey, Fisher, & Everlove, 2009). There are many different ways that students learn collaboratively—from brief partner talks, like Think-Pair-Share, to longer productive group tasks that the whole class is doing while the teacher moves from group to group, clarifying information and providing guided instruction (Lapp, Fisher, & Wolsey, 2009).

Students don't automatically know how to collaborate. They may have collaborated in the past but not with the current content and perhaps not with their current peer group. They need to be taught how to collaborate and what each of their teachers expects in terms of group work. It's not fair to ask students to collaborate in class if they have not been taught how to do so.

As part of learning how to collaborate, students need to be taught to discuss topics in ways that keep the group moving forward. This is especially true because we expect groups to meet with productive failure (Kapur, 2008). This is a state of learning that we actively strive for and is based on the reminder that one learns from one's mistakes. We have noticed that when the task is too easy, groups typically divide the work and go their separate ways until they meet again to assemble the pieces. Ideally, we want the task to be difficult enough so students have a reason to talk with one another to resolve their confusions. However, this is also likely to bring on moments of argument and debate. As we remind them, "It's OK to disagree. It's not OK to be disagreeable."

Accountable talk, described by Michaels, O'Connor, and Resnick (2008) as the academic discourse of learners as they discuss, clarify, question, provide evidence, disagree, and develop solutions, should be the given in the classroom. If it were, then the speaking and listening standards identified in the Common Core State Standards would be of little concern:

> Speaking and Listening standards require students to develop a range of broadly useful oral communication and interpersonal skills. Students must learn to work together, express and listen carefully to ideas, integrate

information from oral, visual, quantitative, and media sources, evaluate what they hear, use media and visual displays strategically to help achieve communicative purposes, and adapt speech to context and task. (NGA & CCSSO, 2010a, p. 8)

Accountable talk has three main components: Everyone is accountable to the classroom community, to the knowledge base, and to reasoned logic. Students can be taught the various ways that they can report on the ideas of others and extend the ideas of others with their own. For example, students can be prompted to make a list of ways to ensure that the words are their own, such as, "Can you put the author's ideas into your own words?" and "Tell more about that." Often, learning the procedures of accountable talk involves a discussion prompt that allows students to carry on a conversation with a partner in which they encourage each other to elaborate on an idea. When students know how to work in a group, the selected text can be more difficult than one that the individual students might read alone.

One of the ways that we help students learn the language of accountable talk is through sentence frames. For example, the following frames were used to provide students with examples that they could use when talking with their group members:

- I agree that ____, a point that needs emphasizing because so many people believe that ____.
- Although I concede that ____, I still insist that ____.
- Although I don't agree that, I do recognize that ____.
- The evidence shows that ____.
- My own view, however, is that ____.

There are a number of different group tasks that involve reading, such as reciprocal teaching, book clubs and literature circles, blogs and online book reviews, collaborative strategic reading, ReQuest, and jigsaws (e.g., Frey et al., 2009), many of which are explored further in Chapter 5. Our point here is that text selection should be based, in part, on how the text is going to be used.

As an example of the power of collaboration to provide access to more complex texts, consider this exchange among a group of 10th graders in their biology class. The class was studying ecology and had read a section of a book focused on flow of energy in the ecosystem.

Duane: I have a question. I read the part about the food chain representing energy transfer, but does it always have to go from producer to herbivore?

Paige: I think that it was just an example that there can be lots of steps in a food chain.

Cody: Yeah, I agree. The figure on page 43 has a food chain, going from producer to herbivore to omnivore to carnivore. I know that the carnivore, the snake on that page, isn't going to eat the plant or probably the grasshopper, so I think it works for this example.

Duane: But does it always have to be that way?

Paige: I don't think so. Like some omnivores eat plants and insects, so it could skip the grasshopper from that picture. The mouse could eat the plant or the grasshopper.

Cody: And some animals really do eat just about anything. I'm thinking of crows and pigs. They eat whatever they can get. So they would have a lot of arrows coming to them and then some things that eat them.

Paige: I think the bears are omnivores, too. But when I went to the zoo, they said that some bears are pretty much only carnivores, and others are pretty much only herbivores. The guide said that it really depends on what food sources are available in their habitat.

Individual Tasks

When students are expected to engage with a text individually, the text selection should not be easy, but it also should not be so difficult that the student is paralyzed by the task. The problem is that the same text is not likely to be appropriate for all of the students in a given class at the same moment in time. When teachers assign a whole-class text for independent reading, some students struggle and fail while others waste time and get bored. It doesn't matter how good or grade-level–appropriate the text is, it will not be a perfect match for every student without instructional interventions. *Shiloh* by Phyllis Reynolds Naylor (1991) is a fantastic book for many students, but we have yet to find an entire class of students who can and want to read that book at the same point in the year.

The Common Core State Standards provide a list of grade-level text exemplars but not a required reading list. The authors of the standards selected the phrase *text exemplars* not *required reading*, and teachers should take this to heart. In doing so, teachers can and should select texts that are more culturally diverse and representative of the larger world. We are reminded that the literature that students read should serve as both a mirror, in which they can see themselves, their families, and their communities, and a window, in which they can meet people who are very different from them (Cullinan, 1989). Having said that, the message is clear: Students should be taught to read increasingly complex texts and supported in that learning. There is nothing in the Common Core State Standards that says that all students have to individually read the same text at the same time.

For independent reading, students should be encouraged to read books that are challenging but not frustrating, but those are not the only texts that students should read. They should read increasingly complex texts with their peers and be exposed to even more complex texts through teacher modeling. As we discussed in the section on motivation, one way to do this is through themes or essential questions. The challenge with questions or themes is that they too often give away the information in the text. When they are broad enough to ensure that students see connections between ideas and not so specific that they remove the inquiry for readers, themes and questions can be used to guide text selection matched to the text. For example, when investigating the question "What is normal, anyway?" different students read different books to gain an understanding of some aspect of the issue (see Table 4.3 for a sample of texts on this topic). They then wrote essays in response to the question, sharing their understanding of the text along the way. This question was not so specific as to ruin the reading or give away the plot.

The key to this approach is to help students find the right independent text. When students are matched with appropriate texts for independent reading, they read more complex texts. For example, Genemo selected *My Stroke of Insight: A Brain Scientist's Personal Journey* by Jill Bolte Taylor (2006) and learned a great deal about a woman who survived a

Table 4.3 Texts That Address the Question "What Is Normal, Anyway?"

- Anderson, L.H. (1999). *Speak*. New York: Farrar, Straus & Giroux.
- Bauby, J. (1997). *The diving bell and the butterfly: A memoir of life in death* (J. Leggatt, Trans.). New York: Alfred A. Knopf.
- Haddon, M. (2003). *The curious incident of the dog in the night-time*. New York: Doubleday.
- Kesey, K. (1962). *One flew over the cuckoo's nest*. New York: Viking.
- Morrison, T. (1987). *Beloved*. New York: Alfred A. Knopf.
- Porter, R. (2002). *Madness: A brief history*. New York: Oxford University Press.
- Skloot, R. (2010). *The immortal life of Henrietta Lacks*. New York: Crown.
- Taylor, J.B. (2006). *My stroke of insight: A brain scientist's personal journey*. New York: Viking.

significant stroke and had to relearn to take care of herself. Seyo selected *The Immortal Life of Henrietta Lacks* by Rebecca Skloot (2010) and learned about the woman who donated, without her knowledge, cells that are still used in cancer research today. Abdurashid selected *One Flew Over the Cuckoo's Nest* by Ken Kesey (1962) and delved into life in a mental hospital. Had the teacher selected one text for all students, none of them would have been as challenged as they were by their independent reading. When we assign whole-class readings, we often undershoot the readers and fail to propel them further (Lapp & Fisher, 2009).

Exploring the Question

The types of questions that teachers ask influence how students read. When asked a series of recall questions, students will focus their reading on details that will allow them to respond to questions about facts. Alternatively, when asked questions that require evaluation or synthesis, students' reading changes, and they focus their attention on global issues and compare that with their own thinking. The following two examples illustrate this difference.

Over the course of the semester, Morgan had been exclusively asked questions that required her to recall details and events from *The Hunger Games* (Collins, 2008). For example, she had been asked, "When did the story take place?" "Where did the story take place?" and "What happened when Katniss first met Gale?" As a result, Morgan became a reader who lacked the critical thinking skills required to respond to the question,

"What would it take, in terms of social changes in a society, for a brutal competition like this to occur?" She floundered with that question and instead retold the story line again from the text, unable to connect this story to the content of her government class.

In another school, Jessie had participated in a number of discussions about texts and had had an opportunity to respond to a broader range of questions that tapped into her critical thinking skills: "What might have happened if Peeta had not given Katniss bread?" and "Was there anything that puzzled you in this chapter?" When Jessie was asked the same question about the social changes that could create *The Hunger Games*, she responded with a series of possible events, some based on her extrapolation from the text ("There would probably have been a war."), some from her experience ("I think that the power of government would have to change. I don't think that this could happen in a democracy."), and still others related to her discipline-specific knowledge from her government class:

> I can see the link between these games and the ones held at the Coliseum in ancient Rome. It's the idea of 'bread and circuses' to distract the masses from what's really wrong with their government. Even the name of the country—Panem—means bread in Latin. *Panem et circenses*. Bread and circuses. A society has to be willing to give itself over to entertainment rather than pay attention to governance.

Types of Questions Matter

Of course, teachers have known about question types and the skills required to answer different types of questions for years. Who hasn't heard of Bloom's taxonomy (Bloom, Engelhart, Furst, Hill, & Krathwohl, 1956) and the levels of *knowledge, comprehension, application, analysis, synthesis,* and *evaluation*? We are also interested in the revision of Bloom's taxonomy for the 21st century (Anderson & Krathwohl, 2001), focusing on the terms *remembering, understanding, applying, analyzing, evaluating,* and *creating* (see Figure 4.2). We are intrigued with the idea that creating something is the highest order of thinking and that the ability to create rests on the previous types of knowledge.

However, our point here is about questions. What may not be as clear, despite a strong understanding of questioning taxonomies, is the effect

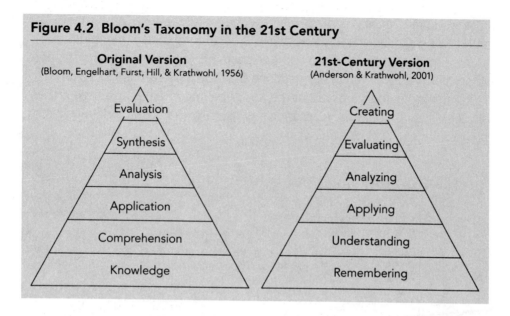

Figure 4.2 Bloom's Taxonomy in the 21st Century

Original Version
(Bloom, Engelhart, Furst, Hill, & Krathwohl, 1956)

Evaluation
Synthesis
Analysis
Application
Comprehension
Knowledge

21st-Century Version
(Anderson & Krathwohl, 2001)

Creating
Evaluating
Analyzing
Applying
Understanding
Remembering

that repeatedly asking certain kinds of questions can have on the reading habits of students. Over time, when they are asked lower order questions, students read for that type of information only. As a cautionary note, we are not suggesting that teachers eliminate remembering, understanding, or applying questions. This information is critical in students' ability to answer complex questions. After all, Jessie would not have been able to answer our question if she hadn't already had a basic understanding of the text, but she also needed to be asked questions that invited her to analyze and evaluate to make the kinds of sophisticated connections using other sources of knowledge to support her claims.

Shifting Expectations

Success on the Common Core State Standards requires students to provide evidence from the text and justify their responses. This may be a new expectation for students who are accustomed to making personal connections with the text and to not being required to support their conclusions or justify their opinions (Fisher, Frey, & Lapp, 2012). Of course, students need practice with this if they are going to succeed in meeting these high expectations. As we have said before, the types of questions that students are asked will guide how they read the text. With that in mind, we have developed a number of questions that can get students started in thinking about the text and in justifying their answers. In Table 4.4, we provide a number of questions that teachers can use to invite students into discussions about the text. The major departure here is that students have to be reminded to provide justifications and evidence from the text for each of their answers.

Table 4.4 Questions About Texts

The story	• What happens in the story? • What happens first/next/last? • Were you able to predict the ending? • What other ways might the story have ended? • What will probably happen next? Why do you think this? • What might have happened if [a certain action] had not taken place? • What is the most important part of the story? What makes you think this? • Under a heading (e.g., People, Animals, Places, Things), list important words from the text.
Setting	• Where does the story take place? • Why does this setting work? • What is the place like? • Do you know of a place like this? • When does the story take place: in the past, present, or future? • Which part of the story best describes the setting? • What words does the author use to describe the setting?
Author	• What do you know about the author? • Why do you think the author wrote the book? • What is the author trying to tell you in the book? • What does this book tell us about the author? • What sorts of things does your author like to dislike (e.g., people, places, behavior, feelings)? • What did the author have to know about to write this book?
Characters	• Who are the main characters in the story? • (Choose one character.) Why is this character important in the story? • Do you know anyone like this character? • Do any of the characters change? • Why do they behave as they do? • How are the characters different/alike? • Are people really like these characters? • Is the behavior of a particular character right or wrong? • What lesson does the character learn in the story?
Basic questions	• Was there anything you liked about this book? • What especially caught your attention? • What would you have liked more of? • Was there anything you disliked? • Were there parts that bored you? • Was there anything that puzzled you? • Was there anything that you thought was strange? • Was there anything that completely surprised you?

(continued)

Table 4.4 Questions About Texts (continued)

General questions	• When you first saw the book, what kind of book did you think it was going to be? What made you think this? • Now that you've finished reading the book, is it as you expected? • Have you read other books like this one? How is it the same or different? • While you were reading, or now when you think about it, were there words, phrases, or other things to do with the language that you liked or didn't like? • Have you noticed anything special about how language is used in this book? • If the writer asked you what could be improved in the book, what would you say? • If you had written this book, how would you have made it better? • Has anything that happened in this book ever happened to you? • What parts in the book seem to you to be the most true to life? • Did the book make you think differently about your own similar experience? • When you were reading, did you see the story happening in your imagination? • Which details or passages helped you see it best? • Which passages stay in your mind most vividly? • We've listened to one another's thoughts and heard all sorts of thing that each of us has noticed. Are you surprised by anything that someone else said? • Has anyone said anything that has changed your mind about this book or helped you understand it better? • What things that other people said struck you the most? • How long did it take the story to happen? • Did we find out about the story because of the order in which the events actually happened? • Do you always tell a story in sequential order? Why, or why not? • Where did the story happen? • Could it just as well have been set anywhere? • Did you think about the setting as you were reading? • Are there passages in the book that are especially about the place where the story is set? • Which character interested you the most? Why? • Is that character the most important in the story? Or is it really about someone else? • Was there a character you did not like? Why? • Did any of the characters remind you of people you know or characters from other books? • Who is narrating the story? How do we know? • Is the story told in first person or third person? • What does the person telling the story think about the characters? • Do you think he/she likes them? How do you know? • Think of yourself as a spectator. Through whose eyes did you see the story? • Did you only see what one character in the story saw, or did you sometimes see the story through another character? (Were you inside the head of one character or a number of characters?) • When you were reading the story, did you feel like it was happening now, or did you feel like it had happened in the past and was being remembered? What in the writing made you feel this way? • Did you feel as though you were an observer, watching what was happening but not a part of the action? If you were an observer, where were you watching from? Can you tell me places in the book where you felt that way?

Note. From "Asking Questions That Prompt Discussion," by D. Fisher and N. Frey, 2011, *Principal Leadership*, 12(3), p. 60. Copyright 2011 by the National Association of Secondary School Principals. Adapted with permission.

Interesting, when teachers use these types of questions with students and press for evidence and justification, students' questions of one another also change. Students begin to phrase questions to peers similarly to those asked by their teachers. Their conversations become more than amateur interactions about texts, as they use accountable talk to fuel their discussions. Their group interactions serve to apprentice them to the type of thinking required of experts.

As an example, consider the following discussion that a group of students had about the book *Night* by Elie Wiesel (1972). They were talking about the reasons the Jewish people in this book did not fight back right away and, rather, went along with the plans for their relocation.

Marla: I don't think that they really thought that it would be that bad. I mean, who would have imagined that? But did you find something in the text that really shows that? We need more evidence.

Deon: Yeah, like it says right here, "Annihilate an entire people? Wipe out a population dispersed throughout so many nations? So many millions of people! By what means? In the middle of the twentieth century?" [p. 8]. They just didn't think it was possible. I agree with you.

Jessica: Yeah, I agree, too. But I also think that it was because life was kinda normal. Yeah, they moved and lost things. But at first their life seemed kinda normal. See right here where it says, "Little by little life returned to 'normal.' The barbed wire that encircled us like a wall did not fill us with real fear. In fact, we felt this was not a bad thing; we were entirely among ourselves" [p. 11].

Deon: Exactly, that's why they didn't fight. They couldn't imagine things would ever be like they turned out, and that their lives got back to normal, well kinda normal, not too bad so that they would fight. There's lots of evidence for this.

This discussion demonstrates the power of the types of questions these students had been asked. Their reading was deeper and focused on the evidence that the author presents. Like their classmates, Marla, Deon, and Jessica learned to focus their reading on a wide range of questions and, in the process, come to understand that they must provide evidence and justification for their responses.

Cautions and Criticisms of Matching Readers With Texts and Tasks

It almost goes without saying that students are diverse and that there is a wide range of skills and interests among students in any classroom. This is a challenge for teachers, and any discussion of text complexity adds to that challenge. Getting to know students is time-consuming, and it's not a perfect science. In the language of research, there isn't great inter-rater reliability between the personal information that two different teachers have about the same student. Thus, matching texts with readers is not a perfect science. Having said that, to ignore the reader would be a significant mistake and would likely result in low expectations for most students and unnecessary struggle for others.

The challenge, really, is to keep all the information about all the students in mind for lesson planning. Teachers have to think about interests, motivations, current skill levels, and attention as they select texts worthy of instruction. Moreover, as we have discussed, each of these factors related to students is malleable. Students change. Their interests change, and their current performance and skills change. As these changes occur, the students need new and different texts to challenge them.

In addition, teachers have to think about how best to use the texts that they have selected. Some texts are better suited for teacher-led activities, others are appropriate for peer discussions, and still others are useful for independent tasks. There isn't a perfect book, but there are good choices for specific readers and specific tasks. This requires a level of knowledge and skill on the part of the teacher. Thankfully, this responsibility has shifted back to teachers. As the authors of the Common Core State Standards so aptly note, "educators will employ professional judgment to match texts to particular students and tasks" (NGA & CCSSO, 2010b, p. 7). It simply is a lot to keep in mind.

Conclusion

Understanding the reader and the task rounds out the process for understanding text complexity. It might be easier, and faster, to rely only on quantitative measures of text difficulty, but this is too problematic to be effective. Readers have to be matched with appropriate texts and tasks (Mesmer, 2008). This is not new. Teachers have been trying to match texts and readers for decades. What is new is the expectation that students should read increasingly complex texts so they are ready for the reading that they will be expected to do in college or as part of their careers. As noted in the Common Core State Standards,

> Despite steady or growing reading demands from various sources, K–12 reading texts have actually trended downward in difficulty in the last half century. Jeanne Chall and her colleagues (Chall, Conard, & Harris, 1977) found a thirteen-year decrease from 1963 to 1975 in the difficulty of grade 1, grade 6, and (especially) grade 11 texts. Extending the period to 1991, Hayes, Wolfer, and Wolfe (1996) found precipitous declines (relative to the period from 1946 to 1962) in average sentence length and vocabulary level in reading textbooks for a variety of grades. (NGA & CCSSO, 2010b, p. 3)

It's time to step it up a bit and teach students to read—and read well. This starts with an understanding of text complexity. Without this understanding, teachers have a hard time figuring out what students need to learn next. When teachers analyze texts for the component parts that increase difficulty, lesson planning and instruction become relevant and worthwhile for building needed student skills. As we have noted, this understanding of text complexity requires attention to quantitative, qualitative, and matching factors. By themselves, none will provide the robust information necessary for changing the state of education and ensuring that every student has the opportunity to participate fully in our democracy.

REFERENCES

Anderson, L.W., & Krathwohl, D.R. (Eds.). (2001). *A taxonomy for learning, teaching, and assessing: A revision of Bloom's taxonomy of educational objectives.* New York: Longman.

Bloom, B.S., Engelhart, M.D., Furst, E.J., Hill, W.H., & Krathwohl, D.R. (Eds.). (1956). *Taxonomy of educational objectives: The classification of educational goals. Handbook I: Cognitive domain.* New York: Longman.

Cromley, J.G., & Azevedo, R. (2007). Testing and refining the direct and inferential mediation model of reading comprehension. *Journal of Educational Psychology, 99*(2), 311–325. doi:10.1037/0022-0663.99.2.311

Cross, D.R., & Paris, S.G. (1988). Developmental and instructional analyses of children's metacognition and reading comprehension. *Journal of Educational Psychology, 80*(2), 131–142. doi:10.1037/0022-0663.80.2.131

Cullinan, B.E. (1989). *Literature and the child* (2nd ed.). San Diego, CA: Harcourt Brace Jovanovich.

Donovan, M.S., & Bransford, J.D. (Eds.). (2005). *How students learn: History, mathematics, and science in the classroom.* Washington, DC: National Academies Press.

Duffy, G.G. (2003). *Explaining reading: A resource for teaching concepts, skills, and strategies.* New York: Guilford.

Ericsson, K.A., & Charness, N. (1994). Expert performance: Its structure and acquisition. *American Psychologist, 49*(8), 725–747. doi:10.1037/0003-066X.49.8.725

Ericsson, K.A., Krampe, R.T., & Tesch-Römer, C. (1993). The role of deliberate practice in the acquisition of expert performance. *Psychological Review, 100*(3), 363–406. doi:10.1037/0033-295X.100.3.363

Fisher, D., & Frey, N. (2011a). Asking questions that prompt discussion. *Principal Leadership, 12*(3), 58–60.

Fisher, D., & Frey, N. (2011b). *The purposeful classroom: How to structure lessons with learning goals in mind.* Alexandria, VA: ASCD.

Fisher, D., Frey, N., & Lapp, D. (2012). *Teaching students to read like detectives: Comprehending, analyzing, and discussing text.* Bloomington, IN: Solution Tree.

Frey, N., Fisher, D., & Everlove, S. (2009). *Productive group work: How to engage students, build teamwork, and promote understanding.* Alexandria, VA: ASCD.

Justice, L.M., Pullen, P.C., & Pence, K. (2008). Influence of verbal and nonverbal references to print on preschoolers' attention to print during storybook reading. *Developmental Psychology, 44*(3), 855–866. doi:10.1037/0012-1649.44.3.855

Kapur, M. (2008). Productive failure. *Cognition and Instruction, 26*(3), 379–424. doi:10.1080/07370000802212669

Kintsch, W., & van Dijk, T.A. (1978). Toward a model of text comprehension and production. *Psychological Review, 85*(5), 363–394. doi:10.1037/0033-295X.85.5.363

Lapp, D., & Fisher, D. (2009). It's all about the book: Motivating teens to read. *Journal of Adolescent & Adult Literacy, 52*(7), 556–561. doi:10.1598/JAAL.52.7.1

Lapp, D., Fisher, D., & Grant, M. (2008). "You can read this text—I'll show you how": Interactive comprehension instruction. *Journal of Adolescent & Adult Literacy, 51*(5), 372–383. doi:10.1598/JAAL.51.5.1

Lapp, D., Fisher, D., & Wolsey, T.D. (2009). *Literacy growth for every child: Differentiated small-group instruction K–6.* New York: Guilford.

McRae, A., & Guthrie, J.T. (2009). Promoting reasons for reading: Teacher practices that impact motivation. In E.H. Hiebert (Ed.), *Reading more, reading better* (pp. 55–76). New York: Guilford.

McVay, J.C., & Kane, M.J. (2011). Why does working memory capacity predict variation in reading comprehension? On the influence of mind wandering and executive attention [Electronic version]. *Journal of Experimental Psychology: General.* Retrieved January 6, 2012, from psycnet.apa.org/psycinfo/2011-19417-001/

Mesmer, H.A.E. (2008). *Tools for matching readers to texts: Research-based practices.* New York: Guilford.

Michaels, S., O'Connor, C., & Resnick, L.B. (2008). Deliberative discourse idealized and realized: Accountable talk in the classroom and in civic life. *Studies in Philosophy and Education, 27*(4), 283–297. doi:10.1007/s11217-007-9071-1

National Governors Association Center for Best Practices & Council of Chief State School Officers. (2010a). *Common Core State Standards for English language arts and literacy in history/social studies, science, and technical subjects.* Washington, DC: Authors. Retrieved January 7, 2012, from www.corestandards.org/assets/ CCSSI_ELA%20Standards.pdf

National Governors Association Center for Best Practices & Council of Chief State School Officers. (2010b). *Common Core State Standards for English language arts and literacy in history/social studies, science, and technical subjects: Appendix A: Research supporting key elements of the standards and glossary of key terms.* Washington, DC: Authors. Retrieved January 7, 2012, from www.corestandards. org/assets/Appendix_A.pdf

RAND Reading Study Group. (2002). *Reading for understanding: Toward an R&D program in reading comprehension.* Santa Monica, CA: RAND.

Roller, C.M. (1996). *Variability, not disability: Struggling readers in a workshop classroom.* Newark, DE: International Reading Association.

Rosenblatt, L.M. (2003). Literary theory. In J. Flood, D. Lapp, J.R. Squire, & J.M. Jensen (Eds.), *Handbook of research on teaching the English language arts* (2nd ed., pp. 67–73). Mahwah, NJ: Erlbaum.

Taylor, D. (1990). *Learning denied.* Portsmouth, NH: Heinemann.

Thomas, H.K., Healy, A.F., & Greenberg, S.N. (2007). Familiarization effects for bilingual letter detection involving translation or exact text repetition. *Canadian Journal of Experimental Psychology, 61*(4), 304–315. doi:10.1037/cjep2007030

Wigfield, A., & Guthrie, J.T. (1997). Relations of children's motivation for reading to the amount and breadth of their reading. *Journal of Educational Psychology, 89*(3), 420–432. doi:10.1037/0022-0663.89.3.420

LITERATURE CITED

Aliki. (1997). *My visit to the zoo.* New York: HarperCollins.

Anderson, L.H. (1999). *Speak.* New York: Farrar, Straus & Giroux.

Bauby, J. (1997). *The diving bell and the butterfly: A memoir of life in death* (J. Leggatt, Trans.). New York: Alfred A. Knopf.

Collins, S. (2008). *The hunger games.* New York: Scholastic.

Cronin, D. (2000). *Click, clack, moo: Cows that type.* New York: Simon & Schuster.

Gibbons, G. (1991). *Zoo.* New York: HarperTrophy.

Haddon, M. (2003). *The curious incident of the dog in the night-time.* New York: Doubleday.

Hansten, P.D., & Horn, J.R. (2011). *Drug interactions analysis and management 2011* (6th ed.). St. Louis, MO: Lippincott Williams & Wilkins.

Ipcizade, C. (2008). *'Twas the day before Zoo Day.* Mt. Pleasant, SC: Sylvan Dell.

Kesey, K. (1962). *One flew over the cuckoo's nest.* New York: Viking.

Koegel, T.J. (2010). *The exceptional presenter goes virtual: Take command of your message, create an "in-person" experience and captivate any remote audience.* Austin, TX: Greenleaf.

Konigsburg, E.L. (1967). *From the mixed-up files of Mrs. Basil E. Frankweiler.* New York: Bantam Doubleday Dell.

Liebman, D. (2003). *I want to be a zookeeper.* Buffalo, NY: Firefly.

Morrison, T. (1987). *Beloved.* New York: Alfred A. Knopf.

Naylor, P.R. (1991). *Shiloh.* New York: Bantam Doubleday Dell.

Porter, R. (2002). *Madness: A brief history.* New York: Oxford University Press.

Silverman, H.M. (2010). *The pill book* (14th ed.). New York: Bantam.

Skloot, R. (2010). *The immortal life of Henrietta Lacks.* New York: Crown.

Taylor, J.B. (2006). *My stroke of insight: A brain scientist's personal journey.* New York: Viking.

Wiesel, E. (1972). *Night.* New York: Hill and Wang.

CHAPTER 5

A Close Reading of Complex Texts

The majority of this book has been devoted to analyzing texts and determining the ways in which a given text is complex. We have focused on quantitative and qualitative factors of text complexity as well as the match among the text, the reader, and the task. We now turn our attention to how a text can be used in the classroom. The title of this chapter is important: a close reading of complex texts, not assigning complex texts. As we have noted throughout this book, simply selecting hard books and telling students to read them will not work. Students need to be taught how to read and think about complex texts.

Accordingly, the majority of this chapter focuses on the instruction necessary to scaffold students' understanding of the text. We do not spend a great deal of time focused on independent reading. Suffice it to say that students should be reading widely, building their background knowledge and vocabulary. The books that students read independently should include a wide range of genres and topics. Additionally, students should read for enjoyment, for the sheer pleasure of engaging with a book on a subject of interest. It is essential that our purposes for reading aren't so narrow as to be viewed solely as a school activity, one to be avoided at all costs outside of the classroom.

As students experience high-quality lessons with complex texts, the ones they read independently will become increasingly more complex over time. Teachers cannot leave this to chance. Instead, they should regularly meet with individual students and talk about the books they are reading. In doing so, the teacher can determine if students are applying the skills they have been taught to the books they are reading independently. In addition, these conferences should provide the teacher an opportunity to reflect on the lessons that each student needs to increase the complexity of the texts that can be read independently.

The lessons that are developed for individual students, small groups of students, and the whole class should provide learners with experiences that allow them to delve deeply into the text. This requires a careful reading and often rereading of the same text. As Newkirk (2010) notes, not all texts demand this level of attention, but some texts do. Complex texts often require the reader's attention and invite the reader back to think more deeply about the meaning of the text. As Newkirk states, "We never really 'comprehend' these anchoring passages—we're never done with them; we never consume them. Like sacred texts, they are inexhaustible, continuing to move us, support us, and even surprise us" (p. 11). In other words, complex texts require a close reading.

Close Reading

The idea of close reading is not new. Richards (1929) gave his students poems and did not tell them who wrote them or when. He wanted his students to concentrate on the words on the page and derive the correct meaning from the words themselves, with no preconceived notions about the text or influences from their own lives. One of Richards's students, Empson (1930), developed a theory about criticism that would significantly influence a new literary movement of the time, New Criticism. New Critics paid little attention to the historical setting of the works and focused instead on finding the correct meaning within the text.

However, in practice, readers rarely put aside their own experiences and perspectives. Instead, readers interact with the text based on what they know. The theory that sought to replace the New Criticism approach was reader response theory. As Blau (1993) notes,

> A work of literature is an inert text that can hardly be said to have more than a potential for meaning until it is called into being by a reader who constructs a reading, thereby giving meaning to the text. (p. 4)

Rosenblatt (1978) notes, "The formal elements of the work—style and structure, rhythmic flow—function only as a part of the total literary experience" (p. 7).

According to reader response theory, there are numerous possible interpretations of a text, and an individual's interpretation may change over time. Reading a book at age 21 will likely result in different interpretations compared with reading the same book at 31, 41, or 51. Think of *The Jungle Book* (Kipling, 1913). A young child can appreciate its themes of loyalty and friendship, whereas an adult reader sees the book's anticolonialist message. In addition to experiences, reader response theory suggests that a reader's perspective also influences understanding. Thus, students from different cultural, ethnic, and linguistic backgrounds might interact and interpret a text differently.

In some cases, the misapplication of reader response theory can result in interactions with the text that focus nearly exclusively on the reader to the exclusion of the text. For example, a student might be asked to write an essay in response to a reading in which he or she is encouraged to "rewrite the ending to include an outcome you would prefer." This is really no improvement over the New Criticism theorists who focus exclusively on the text and exclude the reader altogether.

When this balance is tipped too far in one direction or the other, the reader suffers. There is meaning in the text. As authors, we intend to share some of our ideas through writing. Yet, those ideas are interpreted by readers based on their experiences and beliefs. Importantly, the reader response theory does not focus exclusively on the reader but rather the transaction between the reader and the text. As Rosenblatt (1995) suggests, "The reader must remain faithful to the author's text and must be alert to the potential clues concerning character and motive" (p. 11). Rosenblatt worried that readers might ignore elements in a text and fail to realize that they are "imputing to the author views unjustified by the text" (p. 11).

The Common Core State Standards suggest that students should consider the sociopolitical and historical context of the text while focusing on what the author actually says. The adoption of new standards and the focus on text complexity will not push the field backward to an exclusive focus on the text and the one right way to think about what the author says. In fact, we are hopeful that quite the opposite will occur. Close examination of complex texts is exactly what is required for critical literacy. Freebody and Luke (1990) describe four roles that are necessary for every reader to assume:

1. *Code breaker:* Understanding the text at the surface level (i.e., alphabetic, structural)

2. *Meaning maker:* Comprehending the text at the level intended by the author

3. *Text user:* Analyzing the factors that influenced the author and the text, including a historical grounding of the context within which it was written

4. *Text critic:* Understanding that the text is not neutral and that existing biases inform calls to action

Students reach the deep understanding necessary for text criticism by progressing through these stages of analysis. To stop prematurely, locating understanding only through the first two roles, is to shortchange readers by limiting their view of themselves merely as consumers of text and nothing more.

However, adoption of new standards and the focus on text complexity will require that students understand what the author says and be able to defend their opinions and ideas with evidence from the text. In other words, lessons of the future must provide the balance that we think Rosenblatt was looking for. To accomplish this, several key points deserve attention, including the use of short passages, rereading, reading with a pencil, noticing things that are confusing, discussing the text with others, and responding to text-dependent questions.

Selecting Short, Worthy Passages

When students are introduced to a procedure, skill, or strategy through close reading, it's wise to use a short piece of text. Constraining the amount of text under investigation helps students see how to apply the skill or strategy and limits the amount of time required to teach that skill or strategy. To really understand a text, the reader will likely have to read it more than once. Long pieces of text make it hard for students to reread within the context of the classroom. We aren't suggesting that students should only read short pieces of text. Students should learn to apply their close reading techniques as needed. Remember that not all texts require a close reading. Sometimes we read for pleasure, and other times we read to find a specific piece of information. When we read to really understand something, whether narrative or informational text, we need to read closely enough to make sense of what the author is saying and then compare that with our own experiences and beliefs. Close reading does not mean that the reader has to agree with everything that is read, but the reader should understand what he or she is reading.

In terms of text selection, the recommendation to use short pieces of text for lessons on close reading does not mean that teachers only use short stories or news. There are often specific passages from a longer piece of text that deserve a close reading. For example, this excerpt from "The Nose" by Nikolai Gogol (1836/1972) was used for a close reading lesson. Mr. Taylor provided his students with this passage and asked them to notice what was confusing about it. As they read independently, they took notes about the confusing parts.

> An extraordinarily strange thing happened in St. Petersburg on 25 March. Ivan Yakovlevich, a barber who lived on Voznesensky Avenue (his surname has got lost and all that his shop-front signboard shows is a gentleman with a lathered cheek and the inscription 'We also let blood'), woke up rather early one morning and smelt hot bread. As he sat up in bed he saw his wife, who was a quite respectable lady and a great coffee-drinker, taking some freshly baked rolls out of the oven.
>
> 'I don't want any coffee today, Praskovya Osipovna,' said Ivan Yakovlevich. 'I'll make do with some hot rolls and onion instead.' (Here I must explain that Ivan Yakovlevich would really have liked to have had some coffee as well, but knew it was quite out of the question to expect both coffee *and* rolls, since Praskovya Osipovna did not take very kindly to these whims of his.) 'Let the old fool have his bread, I don't mind,' she thought. 'That means extra coffee for me!' And she threw a roll on to the table.
>
> Ivan pulled his frock-coat over his nightshirt for decency's sake, sat down at the table, poured out some salt, peeled two onions, took a knife and with a determined expression on his face started cutting one of the rolls.
>
> When he had sliced the roll in two, he peered into the middle and was amazed to see something white there. Ivan carefully picked at it with his knife, and felt it with his finger. 'Quite thick,' he said to himself. 'What on earth can it be?'
>
> He poked two fingers in and pulled out—a nose! (p. 42)

The majority of students thought that some of the words were confusing, but as Arriana said, "It's not like they're too hard to understand what's going on. It's just that I want to know what the author is really saying. Like, what is a lathered cheek?" Jasmine added, "And what about the frock-coat? Is that a special kinda coat? Maybe I need one," which prompted giggles from the other students. However, the rational answer that Mr. Taylor was looking for came from Brandi, who said, "Now, if they cooked the nose in the bread, it really wouldn't look like a nose now, would it?"

Mr. Taylor listens closely to his students because what they say (and don't say) gives him insight into what they are having difficulty understanding. In turn, he rapidly makes some decisions about what he will model. He noticed that they were stymied by the language ("lathered cheek" and "frock-coat") and that they missed an important clue that sets this story in time ("'We let blood'"). At this point, Mr. Taylor modeled his thinking, noting that *letting blood* means that small quantities of blood used to be withdrawn in the belief that this would prevent or treat an illness. In his words, "blood-letting is an older practice that lasted through most of the 1800s, which tells me that this story is taking place a long time ago. People used to go to the barbershop for medical procedures like this."

He also noted that there was little conversation about the startling fact that a nose appeared in a bread roll. He then shared some information about magical realism, the tradition in literature that allows for some magical thing to happen in an otherwise conventional story. As Strecher (1999) notes, magical realism is "what happens when a highly detailed, realistic setting is invaded by something too strange to believe" (p. 267). After reading the last sentence, Mr. Taylor said, "It seemed like such an ordinary morning, and then this!" He asked students to reread the selected passage with an understanding of this literary tradition. "Notice how startled this makes you feel. When you're done, let's talk about it some more."

Rereading

It isn't uncommon for students to read a passage once, quickly and rather superficially, and then announce, "I'm done!" Sophisticated readers understand that the nature of some texts requires that they be read more than once. Even with less dense text, it is essential to glean the details at both the explicit and implicit levels to fully understand the reading. First and foremost, close reading requires a willingness to return to the text to read part or even all of it more than once.

Even young students can engage in the kind of rereading that helps them notice important details, as well as the more subtle characteristics of things like tone and voice. A group of Ms. Anaya's second graders was reading *26 Fairmount Avenue*, a recounting of author Tomie dePaola's (1999) early childhood as his family built a house. In one chapter, he tells his readers about going to kindergarten.

Ms. Anaya: We've talked before about how we think Tomie is pretty funny, even though other people don't always appreciate it. Can you find an example of that in this chapter?

Marlon: Ooh, I know, it was...

Ms. Anaya: Wait, Marlon. Be sure everyone has a chance to look first. Do you have your page ready?

Marlon: Oh, yeah, I forgot. [slowly turning pages of the book] It's in here somewhere. Yep, here it is!

Ms. Anaya: Excellent. Put your finger on that example. [to the other students] Get your finger ready, too, so we can talk about it. [The other children join in.] OK, Marlon, give us your example.

Marlon: When he left kindergarten and walked straight home!

Ms. Anaya: Tell us more about that. Help us get on the right page so we can read it with you.

Marlon: Start on page 34 where it says, "I went up to a lady who looked like she might be the teacher."

Ms. Anaya: Where should we stop?

Marlon: On the next page. The last sentence is, "And I walked right out of the school and all the way home."

Ms. Anaya: [to the other children] Now, before we talk about it, reread that section to yourself, then Marlon can explain his thinking.

Ms. Anaya's students have learned how to use examples from the text and to let their classmates know in advance what passage they will be speaking about. By slowing down the conversation just a bit, Ms. Anaya creates a space for students to reread in advance of discussion:

> One of the things I've noticed is that they seem to be getting better at listening to each other. The rereading gets them paying attention to someone else's ideas, instead of only thinking about what they are going to say next.

Reading With a Pencil

Close reading requires reading with a pencil. Well, perhaps not literally a pencil, but with some note-making device. As readers, most of us want to write in or on the text. We make margin notes, we highlight, we underline, all because the act of making notes helps us pay attention to the text and allows us to return to the text later when we want to provide evidence. Yet, writing in books in school is frowned upon, so we have to teach students other ways to read with a pencil. This might include traditional lined paper notes, interactive graphic organizers, or electronic notes. The system of note-taking is less important, but the fact that students read and take notes during a close reading is important.

The notes in a book can reveal much about the reader. Edgar Allan Poe, himself an unapologetic penciler, wrote, "in the *marginalia*, too, we talk only to ourselves; we therefore talk freshly—boldly—originally—with *abandonment*—without conceit" (p. 483, 1844/1988). The practice of making notes to oneself during a reading was for centuries a widespread practice but fell out of favor in the 20th century as public libraries became common. To write in a book was thought to sully it somehow. To be sure, writing in a text that doesn't belong to you isn't looked on kindly. Yet, in the process of protecting the public books, we forgot about the gains to be had from writing in one that belongs to us alone.

In their seminal text, *How to Read a Book* (1940/1972), Adler and Van Doren lay out a case for engaging in repeated readings with accompanying annotation:

> Why is marking a book indispensable to reading it? First, it keeps you awake—not merely conscious, but wide awake. Second, reading, if it is active, is thinking, and thinking tends to express itself in words, spoken or written. The person who says he knows what he thinks but cannot express it usually does not know what he thinks. Third, writing your reactions down helps you to remember the thoughts of the author. (p. 49)

The authors go on to describe the most common annotation marks:

- *Underlining*—of major points; of important or forceful statements.
- *Vertical lines at the margin*—to emphasize a statement already underlined or to point to a passage too long to be underlined.
- *Star, asterisk, or other doodad at the margin*—to be used sparingly, to emphasize the ten or dozen most important statements or passages in the book. You may want to fold a corner of each page on which you make such marks or place a slip of paper between the pages....
- *Numbers in the margin*—to indicate a sequence of points made by the author in developing an argument.

- *Numbers of other pages in the margin*—to indicate where else in the book the author makes the same points, or points relevant to or in contradiction of those here marked; to tie up the ideas in a book, which, though they may be separated by many pages, belong together....
- *Circling of key words or phrases*—This serves much the same function as underlining.
- *Writing in the margin, or at the top or bottom of the page*—to record questions (and perhaps answers) which a passage raises in your mind; to reduce a complicated discussion to a simple statement; to record the sequence of major points right through the book. (pp. 49–50)

Eleventh-grade English teacher Mr. Boulanger asks his students to annotate text as they read short stories. "With the Common Core [State Standards] asking us to up the text complexity, I realized that they needed lots more experience with how to do this," he said. Many of his students are good readers, but they have what Mr. Boulanger calls a "naive understanding" of their ability to hold extensive amounts of information in their minds. "Some of them think that reading is reading, whether it's a novel you're reading at the beach or a scientific paper about an experiment."

At the beginning of the school year, Mr. Boulanger introduced his students to a method of annotation similar to the one described by Adler and Van Doren (1940/1972), and his students now use this method when engaged in close readings. After the class had read the short story "Sonny's Blues" by James Baldwin (1965) for the first time, they returned to the reading, this time examining it more closely for themes. Mr. Boulanger had created a copy of the text with a column for annotated notes on the left side of the pages so students could write on the text. At his direction, they combed the reading to find examples of Baldwin's use of darkness and light as a way to contrast the relationship between the two brothers. The students then discussed this imagery in their table groups:

Khadijah: I underlined right here where he said that "the bright sun deadened his damp dark brown skin" [p. 106] because I could imagine how sickly Sonny must have looked in the outside light.

Paco: That's good, yeah, you're right. I wrote a note to myself about him bein' in the club, and there were jazz musicians. I was thinking 'bout there being a piano there, and the keys are black and white...

Elisa: And you play different notes, like some are sharp, and some are flat.

Khadijah: Sounds like those piano lessons finally paid off for you.

Elisa: [laughs] Yeah, but it's true. I marked this part where the narrator is talking about when the old folks are all together and it's just starting to get dark…

Paco: Yeah, and the kid is scared that things will change, and then it says…wait, I circled it right here…

Elisa: I got it. "And when light fills the room, the child is filled with darkness. He knows that every time this happens, he's moved just a little closer to the darkness outside" [p. 115].

Khadijah: It's like that poem we read, "Nothing gold can stay" [by Robert Frost]. You're a little kid, but you're growing up, and you know that feeling safe and protected is going to go away.

By annotating texts, whether informational, persuasive, or narrative, students learn to slow down their reading to mine the depths of the concepts, arguments, and metaphors used by the writer. Although this practice isn't necessary or even desirable for everything students read, it is important when the information in the text requires close inspection to unlock its meaning.

Noticing Confusing Parts

As part of a close reading, students learn to notice parts of the text that they find confusing. Teachers have taught students to monitor their comprehension for decades, but identifying the specific parts of a text that are confusing requires fairly complex thinking. Like monitoring, noticing is a metacognitive skill, meaning that it is not just thinking but rather thinking about your thinking. This has to be taught. Although most readers know when they have lost the thread of the reading and when they are not understanding what they are reading, most do not know what caused the confusion. Learning to notice is an important, even critical, skill if students are to learn to read complex texts.

There are a number of factors that can cause this confusion. It might be as simple as a single unknown word or as complicated as a big idea that the reader has never considered before. It could be the structure of the sentences or the way referents are or are not provided. It might even be the structure of the text itself. It really doesn't matter what is confusing the reader as long as he or she notices it.

One reason to teach students to notice the confusing parts is to identify what aspects of the text the teacher might subsequently model. In a close reading, students typically encounter the text individually at first. As they read with a pencil and notice what's confusing, the teacher monitors their confusions and makes a determination about what skills or strategies need additional instruction. Often, these misunderstandings become the fodder for teacher modeling. Other times, the misunderstandings are clarified through questioning, as we explore in greater detail later in this chapter. In other words, in a close reading, the teacher should not give away the meaning of the text in advance of the close reading, and the teacher should refrain from front-loading or preteaching vocabulary. Although there is a role for front-loading and preteaching, close readings should allow students to first notice what is confusing so they develop a habit that they can use when they are reading independently. The reading of "The Nose" was an example of this principle. The teacher allowed the students to encounter the text first while he observed and questioned their understanding. He then decided which aspects of the text he would model before returning control to the students and encouraging them to continue reading.

The same is true for students in other grades. For example, fourth graders were introduced to the Carl Sandburg (1970) poem "Fog":

> The fog comes
> on little cat feet.
>
> It sits looking
> over harbor and city
> on silent haunches
> and then moves on. (p. 33)

When several students circled the world *haunches* and wrote a question mark next to it, the teacher knew that she needed to provide guidance. In this case, she used questions to help students understand. For example, she asked, "What is the metaphor our poet uses?" All of the students responded, "A cat!" She then asked, "What does it look like when a cat sits—not lays down and stretches but sits? Show me." As the students moved around and assumed cat-like positions, she said,

> Ah, I see David is on his haunches. Oh, and Leslie. And Mariah. On your haunches, silent. Talk with your partner about the fog and how it might be like a cat, sitting on its haunches and then moving on.

Discussing the Text

Discussions should allow students to engage in purposeful talk, manage their use of academic and domain-specific language and concepts, and provide an opportunity for them to learn about themselves, one another, and the world. Further, the Common Core State Standards describe the expectations for students in discussions, including the following:

- Engage on a variety of grade-level topics in small- and large-group settings with a diverse range of learners.
- Be prepared for the discussion (e.g., complete the reading in advance).
- Follow discussion guidelines and purposes, including specified assigned roles.
- Ask and answer questions, request clarification, furnish evidence and examples, and contribute ideas that enhance the discussion.
- Summarize and synthesize a speaker's main points.

For example, Mr. Raines, a middle school social studies teacher, regularly uses the published debates featured in *USA Today* to foster conversation and discussion. In one lesson, students read one of two editorials on school discipline: the newspaper's position that zero-tolerance policies should be eased or the opposing view of an education leader who argued that schools need to err on the side of safety. The teacher provided students with the following extended-language frame to support their conversations:

> According to this article, a zero-tolerance policy is (necessary/unnecessary) because ___. First, the author states that ___. In addition, the author argues that ___. I agree with the author's claim that ___. However, I disagree with the claim that ___. In my opinion, ___. What's your opinion?

After posting the language frame on the board, Mr. Raines distributed the readings and invited the students to read and highlight notable sections. Students then met with three other classmates who had read the same editorial to discuss the claims and evidence forwarded by the author. After annotating the article, they met with another student who had read the opposing-view editorial. At this point, students drew on the language frames supplied by the teacher to guide their conversations. First, one partner shared the major points made by the writer and weighed in with his or her own opinions, and then the other partner did the same. Once these partner conversations had taken place, the teacher invited the students back as a whole class and led a debate on the pros and cons advanced by the authors.

After a lively discussion on the merits of each argument, the students once again used a language frame for writing. This time, the students each wrote about their own opinion, using key arguments to support their position. In addition, a new language frame required them to acknowledge counterclaims:

> In my opinion, a zero-tolerance policy is (necessary/unnecessary) because ____. First, the author states that ____. In addition, some argue that ____. I agree with the author's claim that ____. It is important to acknowledge that some will argue that ____. While this argument has some merit, it is not as strong because ____. In summary, I believe a zero-tolerance policy is (necessary/ unnecessary) because ____.

Mr. Raines understands that a series of small-group discussions that he constructs will cause students to reread and examine the information in detail as well as more globally. In addition, he positions reading and discussion as necessary prerequisites to more formal composition. "It's hard for them to persuade when they haven't had a chance to do that themselves—or for that matter, to be persuaded. I want them applying their knowledge of the content to understand editorial commentary more deeply," he said.

Asking Text-Dependent Questions

Because novice readers haven't yet fully developed the habit of rereading, teachers use text-dependent questions to prompt students to return to the text. Text-dependent questions are those that can only be answered with evidence from the text. For example, while reading *Diary of a Spider* by Doreen Cronin (2005), the teacher asked a group of second-grade students why the spider would say, "That worked," when they made a "huge sticky web on the water fountain" (p. 8). They had to understand that the seesaw and swing did not work because the spiders were too small to play, but getting a human stuck in a web was really fun for them because the human says, "eeeek!" and tries to get away. Without reading the book carefully and examining the words and pictures, these students would not be able to answer the question because seesaws and swings are supposed to be fun.

It is important to note that text-dependent questions should not be confined only to the literal meaning of the passage; although important, this does not fully capture the deeper meaning of the work. Therefore, text-dependent questions should also challenge students to examine the inferential levels of meaning, such as noting the mood and tone of a piece, the author's purpose, or how the artful choice of words elevates the quality of the reading. In the spider book, the teacher asked, "Why would they have to play at Fly's house from now on?" following the part where the spider's friend, Fly, is caught in the web and has to be rescued by her mom. In this case, the fly and spider are friends, and the parents must have decided that it was safer to play at Fly's house, even though the text does not say that. Without reading the text and understanding the friendship and the accidental trapping in the web, students might talk about the fact that most spiders catch flies to eat, not to be friends.

Later in the book, grandpa lets the spider kid in on the secret of life: "Never fall asleep in a shoe" (p. 26). When asked to make an inference about why that might help a spider lead a "long, happy life" (p. 25), Michael answered, "I had a spider in my shoe. It was really scary." The teacher calmly redirected the students to the text:

Teacher: Michael, remember we're talking about why the grandpa spider would tell the kid spider not to fall asleep in a shoe. Think about it from the spider's perspective.

Michael: Oh, because they might get killed.

Tina: Yeah, because if there is a spider in your shoe, and you put it on, you could squish the spider dead.

A significant portion of the reading standards in the Common Core State Standards, upwards of 80% in most grades, require students to provide evidence from the text in their responses. That's not to mention the fact that students must justify their written responses with evidence from the text if they are to meet the writing standards. As we noted in the previous chapter, students focus their reading based on the types of questions that they are asked. Unfortunately, students are often asked questions that take them away from the text rather than back into it. For example, while reading *Diary of a Spider*, we would not recommend starting the questioning with something like "Have you seen a spider?" or "What do you know about spiders?" In both cases, students would move immediately to their personal experiences rather than what the text offers. Moreover, activating scientific information about spiders would be of little help in understanding the text. Although it is true that knowing something about spiders will help, especially with the humor, as is the case when the spider has dinner with the worms and has to eat leaves and rotten tomatoes, that is not really the author's purpose. When engaged in a close reading, students should be redirected to the text to make meaning. This is the case for all readers, especially those who struggle in school. Asking the right question and redirecting students to the text can develop students' stamina and skills over time.

The use of questioning routines, such as question–answer relationships, questioning the author, or Bloom's taxonomy-oriented questions (see Chapter 4 for a discussion of Bloom's taxonomy), is effective for developing text-dependent questions. Regardless of the system used, the questions should be developed in advance of the lesson to ensure that the discussion regularly guides students back to the reading.

Question–Answer Relationships is an instructional strategy designed to teach students how to locate and formulate answers to questions about a reading. This approach "clarifies how students can approach the task of reading texts and answering questions" (Raphael, 1986, p. 517). This is accomplished by teaching about four types of questions. The first two are explicit questions, meaning that the answer can be found in the text. "Right there" questions contain wording that comes directly from the text, with an answer often found in a single sentence. "Think and search" questions are also derived directly from the text, but the answer must be formulated across more than one sentence. The other two types of questions are implicit, meaning that the answer cannot be located directly in the text and must be formulated by also using what the reader knows. "Author and you" is an implicit question that requires the reader to use both information learned in the text and his or her own background knowledge to answer. The final type of implicit question is "on your own," which requires the reader to use prior knowledge to answer. The text may or may not be needed.

It is helpful to think of these as book and brain questions. "Right there" and "think and search" are book questions because the answers can be found directly in the text. Conversely, "author and you" and "on your own" questions are brain questions because the readers must consider what they know and what they have learned from the reading. In a close reading, the majority of the questions will be book questions. When the teacher is sure that the students understand the text, brain questions can be used to extend students' learning. See Table 5.1 for examples of these questions.

Questioning the author (Beck & McKeown, 2006) requires students to think beyond the words on the page and consider the author's intent for the selection and his or her success at communicating it. The idea of questioning the author is not an invitation to challenge a writer but rather a way to encourage students to return to the text to find evidence. Students examine the author's intent, craft, clarity, or organization. Questioning the author focuses on five main questions:

1. What is the author trying to tell you?

2. Why is the author telling you that?

3. Does the author say it clearly?

4. How could the author have said things more clearly?

5. What would you say instead?

Over time, students should learn to ask these questions themselves as they read a text. As they learn this procedure, the teacher should ask them these questions or variations of them (see Table 5.2). As students read a selection of text (remember that close reading is based on short, worthy passages), they should answer the five questions.

For example, when students read Annie Davis's August 28, 1864, letter to President Lincoln (Young, 2005; see Figure 5.1) asking if she was a free woman or a slave, they used questioning the author to analyze the letter and the text that explained the letter. The text of the letter is not very complex, but the question asked by the writer is. As they engaged in a

Table 5.1 Question–Answer Relationships

Types of Questions	Descriptions	Stems for Question
In the Text (Book Questions)		
Right there	Words in the question and answer are directly stated in the text. It is explicit, and the words or phrases can be found within one sentence.	• How many…? • Who is…? • Where is…? • What is…?
Think and search	Information is in the text, but readers must think and make connections between passages in the text.	• The main idea is…? • What caused…?
In My Head (Brain Questions)		
Author and you	Readers need to think about what they already know, what the author tells them in the text, and how it fits together.	• The author implies…? • The passage suggests…? • The author's attitude is…?
On your own	Requires the reader to use prior knowledge to answer. The text may or may not be needed.	• In your own opinion…? • Based on your experience…? • What would you do if…?

Note. From *After School Content Literacy Project for California* (p. 186), by D. Fisher, N. Frey, and L. Young, 2007, Sacramento: California Department of Education. Copyright 2007 by the California Department of Education.

Table 5.2 Examples of Queries

Initiating	• What is the author trying to say here? • What is the author's message? • What is the author talking about?
Follow-up	• What does the author mean here? • Did the author explain this clearly? • Does this make sense with what the author told us before? • How does this connect with what the author has told us before? • Does the author tell us why? • Why do you think the author tells us this now?
Narrative	• How do things look for this character now? • How has the author let you know that something has changed? • How has the author settled this for us? • Given what the author has already told us about this character, what do you think he's up to?

Note. From *Questioning the Author: An Approach for Enhancing Student Engagement With Text* (p. 45), by I.L. Beck, M.G. McKeown, R.L. Hamilton, and L. Kugan, 1997, Newark, DE: International Reading Association. Copyright 1997 by the International Reading Association.

Figure 5.1 Letter From Annie Davis to Abraham Lincoln

Mr. President

It is my Desire to be free. to go to see my people on the eastern shore. My mistress wont let me you will please let me know if we are free. and what i can do. I write to you for advice. please send me word this week or as soon as possible and oblidge.

Annie Davis, Belair Harford County, MD.

Note. From *Dear Mr. President: Letters to the Oval Office From the Files of the National Archives* (p. 27), by D. Young, 2005, Washington, DC: National Geographic. Copyright 2005 by National Geographic Books. Reprinted with permission.

text-based discussion, the students focused on the letter and understood that Ms. Davis wanted to know if she was legally allowed to go to her family, likely because of the Emancipation Proclamation. They also discussed the fact that she was from Maryland, a border state that was not in rebellion against the United States, and thus the proclamation did not apply to her. The students agreed that Ms. Davis's letter was clear but that the Emancipation Proclamation was confusing and misled a lot of people.

In the next sections, we provide two examples of close reading lessons. The first is a short informational reading for fourth graders. The second is a narrative piece for ninth-grade students. In each lesson, you will see how independent reading, modeling, think-alouds, discussion, and text-based questions are used to lead students through a deeper examination of texts.

Close Reading Up Close in Fourth Grade: "Post-it Notes"

The purpose of this lesson is to engage fourth-grade students in a close reading of an excerpt from an informational book on the history and development of widely used inventions (see Figure 5.2 for the text). Although independent reading is an important component of this lesson, it should be noted that students are supported in their deepening comprehension of the text through a series of instructional moves that are consistent with a gradual release of responsibility framework, including setting the purpose, teacher modeling, guided instruction, and productive group work, as well as independent tasks (Fisher & Frey, 2008).

Figure 5.2 Post-it Notes

By now everyone knows what Post-it brand notes are. They are those great little self-stick notepapers.

Most people have Post-it Notes. Most people use them. Most people love them.

But Post-it Notes were not a planned product. No one got the idea and then stayed up nights to invent it.

A man named Spencer Silver was working in the 3M research laboratories in 1970 trying to find a strong adhesive. Silver developed a new adhesive, but it was even weaker than what 3M already manufactured. It stuck to objects, but could easily be lifted off. It was superweak instead of superstrong.

No one knew what to do with the stuff, but Silver didn't discard it.

Then one Sunday four years later, another 3M scientist named Arthur Fry was singing in his church's choir. He used markers to keep his place in the hymnal, but they kept falling out of the book.

Remembering Silver's adhesive, Fry used some to coat his markers.

Success! With the weak adhesive, the markers stayed in place, yet lifted off without damaging the pages.

3M began distributing Post-it Notes nationwide in 1980—ten years after Silver developed the superweak adhesive. Today they are one of the most popular office products available.

Note. From *Mistakes That Worked: 40 Familiar Inventions and How They Came to Be* (p. 51), by C.F. Jones, 1991, New York: Doubleday. Copyright 1991 by Charlotte Foltz Jones. Reprinted with permission.

Establish the Purpose With Students

Tell students that the purpose of the lesson is to discover how a familiar office product was initially thought to be a failure and to trace its development as a useful item. Although it is likely that students will know what Post-it Notes are, if you are unsure whether they are familiar with them, you can show them an example. However, be careful not to engage in an extended lesson on Post-it Notes, as the point is to encourage students to investigate the text, not to build so much background knowledge that the need to read is significantly diminished.

Introduce the reading, "Post-it Notes" by Charlotte Foltz Jones (1991), and invite the students to read it first to themselves so they can trace the history of this product. Remind them that if they come to an unfamiliar word, they should look inside the word (structural analysis) for familiar portions, and outside the word (contextual analysis) for clues to its meaning. Ask the students to list words they figured out using this approach, as well as words they are still stuck on.

First Reading: Students Read Independently

As students read, target specific students who may need more assistance with making meaning of the text. Encourage all of the students to make notes to themselves about the major events, and observe their silent reading closely as you watch for signs of difficulty. Encourage the students to circle or underline words, phrases, or sentences that are unclear to them.

First Discussion: Partner Talk to Check Meaning

After students have finished the initial reading, ask them to turn to a partner to describe one surprising fact that they learned about the invention of Post-it Notes, using this language frame: "I was amazed to learn that ___!" Ask the students to write their amazing fact and their partner's in their notes for the reading, as these will be used in the discussion.

Second Discussion: Assessing for Understanding and Confusions

Invite the students to share their amazing facts and those of their partners. This will provide initial insight into what portions of the text students have understood. Ask them what words or phrases are unfamiliar or unclear to them and how they attempted to resolve them. Note the students' responses, as these will guide you regarding what should be modeled.

Second Reading: Teacher-Led Shared Reading and Think-Aloud

Explain to students that you will read the selection aloud to them while they follow along silently with their own copy of the text. Tell them that from time to time, you will explain your thinking to them as you resolve difficult words using structural and contextual clues. As you read the passage, orient the students to where you are in the text so they are tracking the correct part.

The following are possible think-alouds for this text:

- *Paragraph 4:* "'Silver developed a new adhesive, but it was even weaker than what 3M already manufactured.' There are two words I'm not sure of in that sentence: *adhesive* and *manufactured*. I'll keep reading until the end of the paragraph to see if I can figure out what they mean." Reread the entire paragraph. "I can see two clues in the next sentence that give me a hint about what *adhesive* might mean. The author says, 'It stuck to objects,' and that it was 'superweak instead of superstrong.' That gives me a hint that *adhesive* means something that sticks. At first, I wasn't sure I knew what *manufactured* meant, but then I reread the previous sentence and reminded myself that he worked in a laboratory. I realized that his job was to make things. When I substitute *sticky stuff* for *adhesive* and *made* for *manufactured,* the sentence makes sense." Reread the target sentence using the substituted terms. "I used a context clue to figure that word out."

- *Paragraphs 7 and 8:* "'Fry used some to coat his markers.' Did he put a jacket on his markers? That doesn't make any sense. I'll keep reading. 'Success! With the weak adhesive, the markers stayed in place, yet lifted off without damaging the pages.' I'm still struggling with the word *coat,* but now I see that it's used as a verb in that sentence instead of a noun. So, I know it can't mean that it's something you wear. In this sentence, it seems like *coat* means to cover." Reread the sentence, substituting *cover* for *coat.* "Yes, that seems to make sense."

After finishing the shared reading of the entire passage, transition students to a discussion using a series of text-dependent questions.

Third Discussion: Text-Dependent Questions

Keep in mind that the purposes of text-dependent questions are to prompt rereading, encourage the use of textual evidence to support answers, and deepen comprehension using analytic processes. To aid in this analysis, initial questions should be designed to highlight the explicit meaning of the text. However, it is important not to stop there but to progress toward a more challenging and implicit meaning. We provide evidence from the text to anticipate student responses (in practice, the discussion is far richer):

Question 1: Post-it Notes began as an idea that didn't work but then became a very useful product. What was the sequence of events that led to this invention? (As students describe the sequence, ask them to furnish evidence from the text. Encourage them to use academic language and vocabulary in their discussion, especially using words that you have highlighted in the shared reading.)

- Spencer Silver worked at 3M research laboratories and developed an adhesive, but it was weak.
- Arthur Fry came up with a good idea, using Spencer's adhesive to "coat his markers" (para. 7). When he saw that "the markers stayed in place, yet lifted off without damaging the pages" (para. 8), he found a new way to use the adhesive.

Question 2: The author tells you twice when Spencer Silver first invented the adhesive that would be used in the Post-it Notes. The first time is in the fourth paragraph, when she tells us it was 1970. Then, she tells us the same information again later in a different way. How did you figure out the answer?

- In paragraph 9, it says, "in 1980—ten years after Silver developed the superweak adhesive." So, he developed it in 1970.

Question 3: Do you believe the author has a positive or a negative view of Post-it Notes and its inventors? What words or phrases lead you to believe that?

- She uses words and phrases such as "great" (para. 1) and "love them" (para. 2).
- The author says, "Success!" (para. 8), to describe the moment of invention.

Question 4: What were some of the qualities of the inventors that you can infer from this text? What passages helped you draw these conclusions?

- Arthur was imaginative. He was willing to try new things. "Remembering Silver's adhesive, Fry used some to coat his markers. Success!" (paras. 7–8).
- Spencer was clever. He "was working in the 3M research laboratories" and "developed a new adhesive" (para. 4). That would be almost impossible to do unless you had a lot of knowledge about chemistry.

Journal Writing

Students gather notes for the development of an essay that explains their findings of the investigative question, What does it take to be an inventor? For this journal entry, students write a short summary of the invention of

Post-it Notes and assign at least two characteristics to the inventors, using at least two quotations from the text.

Close Reading Up Close in Ninth Grade: "The Road Not Taken"

The purpose of this lesson is to engage ninth-grade students in a close reading of a popular Robert Frost (1916) poem and analyze it for a deeper meaning than the one commonly interpreted. Many students will be familiar with this poem and typically believe that the poet's message is about individualism and the importance of making decisions that lead one in the direction of one's passions. However, a close reading of the poem reveals a contrary interpretation—that one's life decisions are often capricious and irrational and that they may or may not make such a difference after all.

Although independent reading is an important component of this lesson, it should be noted that students are supported in their deepening comprehension of the poem through a series of instructional moves that are consistent with a gradual release of responsibility framework, including setting the purpose, teacher modeling, guided instruction, and productive group work, as well as independent tasks (Fisher & Frey, 2008).

Establish the Purpose With Students

Tell students that the purpose of the lesson is to discover why Frost called this a "'tricky poem'" and a "'wolf in sheep's clothing'" (Bercovitch, 2003, p. 22). Although it is likely that students will have read this poem in the past, remind them that they are going to look for the poet's more subversive message. Be careful not to engage in an extended lesson on Frost and the poem in advance of the reading, as the point is to encourage students to investigate the text.

Introduce the reading, "The Road Not Taken" by Frost, and invite the students to read it first to themselves so they can familiarize themselves with the poem and its conventional interpretation. Using Figure 5.3, invite them to annotate the text and create notes in the left column, paying attention to the words, phrases, and meter of the poem that contribute to the story unfolding in each stanza.

Figure 5.3 "The Road Not Taken"

Conventional Meaning	The Poem's Text	Subversive Meaning
	Two roads diverged in a yellow wood, And sorry I could not travel both And be one traveler, long I stood And looked down one as far as I could To where it bent in the undergrowth;	
	Then took the other, as just as fair, And having perhaps the better claim, Because it was grassy and wanted wear; Though as for that the passing there Had worn them really about the same,	
	And both that morning equally lay In leaves no step had trodden black. Oh, I kept the first for another day! Yet knowing how way leads on to way, I doubted if I should ever come back.	
	I shall be telling this with a sigh Somewhere ages and ages hence: Two roads diverged in a wood, and I— I took the one less traveled by, And that has made all the difference.	
The Poem's Conventional Interpretation:		The Poem's Subversive Message:

Note. The text in each row is a separate stanza.

First Reading: Students Read Independently

As students read, target specific students who may need more assistance with making meaning of the text. Observe their silent reading closely as you watch for signs of difficulty. Encourage them to circle or underline words, phrases, or sentences that are unclear to them.

First Discussion: Partner Talk to Check Meaning

After students have finished their initial reading, ask them to talk with a partner about the story that unfolds across each stanza. As they discuss their ideas, join groups or listen for discussions that focus on conventional interpretations of this poem:

- *Stanza 1:* The poet establishes the setting of woods in autumn, and the narrator encounters a path that reaches in two different directions.

- *Stanza 2:* The narrator hesitates and looks at both paths, then takes the one that doesn't appear to have been used as frequently.

- *Stanza 3:* The narrator walks down one road and realizes that he won't ever get to see where the other road might have led.

- *Stanza 4:* The narrator knows that although the path he chose is less common, it was the right one for him.

Second Discussion: Assessing for Understanding and Confusions

Invite the students to share their observations and those of their partners. In particular, press the students to provide evidence of their interpretations using the poet's words and phrases, stanza by stanza. It should be expected that their initial interpretation of the text is that this poem supports an individualistic and independent life and praises the unconventional life. This will provide initial insight into what portions of the text students have understood. Ask them about words or phrases that are unfamiliar or unclear and how they attempted to resolve them. Note their responses, as these will guide you as to what should be modeled.

Second Reading: Teacher Modeling of Meter

As you prepare for your modeling, remind the students that poems are often best understood as spoken words and tell them that you are going to read it aloud two times. In this reading, invite the students to follow along in the text and notice how the meter of the poem mirrors the cadence of someone walking, then pausing in the third line, and then walking again. This pattern is repeated in each stanza. After you complete the modeled reading, invite the students to read the poem aloud to their partners in a similar fashion, using the rhythm of the poem (iambic tetrameter).

Third Reading: Thinking Aloud to Locate Clues About the Narrator

Remind the students that Frost called "The Road Not Taken" a "'wolf in sheep's clothing'" and explain that you are going to think aloud as you read, with the intent of finding out more about the narrator. Invite them to follow along as you read:

- *Stanza 1, line 1:* "The first line talks about a 'yellow wood,' which means the poem is set in the fall, but I know that there's often lots of symbolism in poetry. This phrase reminds me about the autumn years of a person's life. I think that the narrator is in his late middle age, so maybe he is about 50 years old."

- *Stanza 1, line 3:* "'And be one traveler, long I stood' tells me that he is alone on this journey because he's using first-person singular pronouns."

- *Stanza 2, line 5:* "The last line in this stanza causes me to wonder about this poem. We said earlier that it was about the glory of making an uncommon decision, but now I notice that he says, that they're 'really about the same.' Is he telling me that it doesn't matter so much which way you choose to go?"

- *Stanza 3, line 5:* "Frost uses the word *doubted* in this line. Again, he makes me think that he's not so sure of his choices after all."

- *Stanza 4, line 1:* "Wow, he uses the word *sigh* here. I'm thinking about the times I sigh. Sometimes it's because I'm sad, but other times it's because I'm glad something is over. I'm confused here because I can't tell which way he means it to be understood."

- *Summary:* "So, here's what I've noted about the narrator. I think he's middle-aged and by himself. I also think that he's not so confident about his choices, like he has some doubt or some regret. By paying attention to the narrator, I am beginning to get to the poem's less obvious message."

After finishing the think-aloud of the poem, transition the students to a discussion by using a series of text-dependent questions. Tell the students that this discussion will focus on uncovering the subversive message and that their annotations should now go in the column to the right of the poem.

Third Discussion: Text-Dependent Questions

Keep in mind that the purposes of text-dependent questions are to prompt rereading, encourage the use of textual evidence to support answers, and deepen comprehension using analytic processes. To aid in this analysis, initial questions should be designed to highlight the explicit meaning of the text. However, it is important not to stop there but to progress toward a more challenging and implicit meaning. We provide evidence from the text to anticipate student responses (in practice, the discussion is far richer):

Question 1: What words or phrases does Frost use to suggest that there's not so much difference after all between the two roads?

- The word *both* in stanzas 1 and 3
- The word *equally* in stanza 3
- "Just as fair" in stanza 2 to describe the roads

Question 2: What words or phrases does Frost use to signal regret?

- The word *sorry* in stanza 1
- "Looked down one as far as I could" in stanza 1 suggests that he tried to see what might be up ahead but couldn't see much.
- "Oh, I kept the first for another day!" in stanza 3 means that he intended to come back. This is confirmed two lines later: "I doubted if I should ever come back."

Question 3: When Frost uses the word *sigh*, do you think he means a sigh of regret or relief? Use evidence from the text to support your opinion.

- In stanza 4, he uses the word *I* twice, with a long (em) dash in between them. "Two roads diverged in a wood, and I— / I took the one less traveled by" sounds like when your voice catches in your throat.
- He uses the word *perhaps* in stanza 2, which suggests that he's not sure of his decision.

Question 4: The last word of the poem is *difference*. Does he mean this as a positive difference or a negative one? Why do you think that?

- He's in his late middle age, and now he's not so sure that the decisions he made as a young man really mattered all that much after all.
- He realizes that the paths weren't all that different from each other.
- He's telling himself the story of how he will describe his life to others, even if it's not completely accurate: "Somewhere ages and

ages hence: / Two roads diverged in a wood, and I— / I took the one less traveled by, / And that has made all the difference" (stanza 4).

Question 5: Readers in the early part of the 20th century liked poems that had inspirational messages, so this poem was viewed conventionally as being about the glory of choosing one's own path. But what is the subversive message of this poem?

- We fool ourselves into believing that our life choices are rational, but in reality, most of them are chance.
- We like to believe that our choices carry us on a path that is better, but in the end, maybe it's not.
- The title of the poem is about the road not taken, not about "the one less traveled by" (stanza 4).

Question 6: Why do you believe so many people incorrectly call this poem "The Road Less Traveled" instead of its correct title?

- Many people would rather cling to the conventional and inspirational message rather than the darker and more subversive one.

Journal Writing

As the discussion comes to a close, ask the students to write in their journals about the contrast between the conventional and subversive messages of this poem, using examples from the text to support each message.

Conclusion

As these two sample lessons suggest, teachers can use complex texts to build students' reading skills. As students become more skilled, they will be able to access increasingly complex texts with their peers and independently. As we argued earlier in this book, teaching students to read and understand complex texts begins with an understanding of what makes a text complex. Teachers, not computers, need to analyze texts and determine the instructional match between the texts and the students. Thankfully, there are a number of resources available for teachers, including quantitative readability formulas and qualitative assessment tools, that can be used in these analyses. In addition, before making a final text selection, teachers need to consider the actual readers as well as the tasks that students will be expected to complete with the text.

Having said that, we must commit to our students and help them read increasingly complex texts and read those texts well. In the past, our profession may have been a bit complacent, waiting for students to develop in their literacy skills. That time is over. If we can put a person on the moon, then we can ensure that students can read about it. If we can create the Internet, then we have the responsibility to ensure that all students can access the information contained therein. And if we expect to solve the problems present in the world today, problems that our ancestors could not have imagined, then we must ensure that students can think deeply, look for evidence, and justify their ideas.

REFERENCES

Adler, M.J., & Van Doren, C. (1972). *How to read a book* (Rev. ed.). New York: Touchstone. (Original work published 1940)

Beck, I.L., & McKeown, M.G. (2006). *Improving comprehension with questioning the author: A fresh and expanded view of a powerful approach.* New York: Scholastic.

Beck, I.L., McKeown, M.G., Hamilton, R.L., & Kucan, L. (1997). *Questioning the author: An approach for enhancing student engagement with text.* Newark, DE: International Reading Association.

Bercovitch, S. (2003). *The Cambridge history of American literature. Vol. 5: Poetry and criticism, 1900–1950.* New York: Cambridge University Press.

Blau, S. (1993). *Building bridges between literary theory and the teaching of literature.* Albany: National Research Center on Literature Teaching and Learning, University at Albany, State University of New York. retrieved January 13, 2012, from www.albany.edu/cela/reports/blaubridges.pdf

Empson, W. (1930). *Seven types of ambiguity.* London: Chatto & Windus.

Fisher, D., & Frey, N. (2008). *Better learning through structured teaching: A framework for the gradual release of responsibility.* Alexandria, VA: Association for Supervision and Curriculum Development.

Fisher, D., Frey, N., & Young, L. (2007). *After school content literacy project for California.* Sacramento: California Department of Education.

Freebody, P., & Luke, A. (1990). Literacies programs: Debates and demands in cultural context. *Prospect: Australian Journal of TESOL, 5*(7), 7–16.

Newkirk, T. (2010). The case for slow reading. *Educational Leadership, 67*(6), 6–11.

Poe, E.A. (1988). *Marginalia.* Charlottesville: University of Virginia Press. (Original work published 1844)

Raphael, T.E. (1986). Teaching children question–answer relationships, revisited. *The Reading Teacher, 39*(6), 516–522.

Richards, I.A. (1929). *Practical criticism: A study of literary judgment.* London: Routledge & Kegan Paul.

Rosenblatt, L.M. (1978). *The reader, the text, the poem: The transactional theory of the literary work*. Carbondale: Southern Illinois University Press.

Rosenblatt, L.M. (1995). *Literature as exploration* (5th ed.). New York: Modern Language Association.

Strecher, M.C. (1999). Magical realism and the search for identity in the fiction of Murakami Haruki. *Journal of Japanese Studies, 25*(2), 263–298.

Young, D. (2005). *Dear Mr. President: Letters to the Oval Office from the files of the National Archives*. Washington, DC: National Geographic.

LITERATURE CITED

Baldwin, J. (1965). Sonny's blues. In *Going to meet the man* (pp. 101–141). New York: Dial.

Cronin, D. (2005). *Diary of a spider*. New York: Joanna Cotler.

dePaola, T. (1999). *26 Fairmount Avenue*. New York: G.P. Putnam's Sons.

Frost, R. (1916). The road not taken. In *Mountain interval* (p. 9). New York: Henry Holt.

Gogol, N. (1972). The nose. In *Diary of a madman and other stories* (R. Wilks, Trans.; pp. 42–70). New York: Penguin. (Original work published 1836)

Jones, C.F. (1991). *Mistakes that worked: 40 familiar inventions and how they came to be*. New York: Doubleday.

Kipling, R. (1913). *The jungle book*. New York: Century.

Sandburg, C. (1970). Fog. In *The complete poems of Carl Sandburg* (Rev. ed.; p. 33). Orlando, FL: Harcourt.

Index

Note. Page numbers followed by *f* and *t* indicate figures and tables, respectively.

Frey, N., 11, 42, 44, 54, 57, 78, 80, 89–90, 95, 97, 121–122, 127
Freytag's Pyramid, 55, 56f
friendly texts. *See* considerate texts
Frost, R., 127
frustration level, 6
Fry, E., 26–27
Fry readability formula, 26–28, 27f, 38t
Furst, E.J., 94

G
genre, 53–55; and readability, 34; types of, 54f
Geraghty, C., 6
Gewertz, C., 8
Gibbons, G., 82
goal setting, and motivation, 80–81
Gogol, N., 109
Goldilocks rule, 5
Gonzalez, N., 64
Graesser, A.C., 1, 28, 30, 32, 34
Grafstein, A., 41
Grant, M., 44, 84, 88
graphic organizers, 43; for topic, 13f
graphics, 57–58
Gray, W.S., 21, 25
Greenberg, S.N., 79
Gunning, T.G., 21, 25, 30
Guthrie, J.T., 79–80

H
Haddon, M., 93
Hamilton, R.L., 121
Hansten, P.D., 73
Hare, V.C., 44
Harris, T.L., 3
Harris-Sharples, S., 68
Harvey, C.A. II, 42
Hayes, D.P., 6
headings, 43
Healy, A.F., 79
Hembree, R., 36
Hemingway, Ernest, 25
Herman, J.L., 36
Hesse, H., 64
Hiebert, E.H., 25, 36–37, 67
Hill, W.H., 94
Hodges, R.E., 3
Hoover, H.D., 36
Horabin, I., 30
Horn, J.R., 73
Hughes, L., 13

hyperbole, 51t

I
imagery, 51t
independent level, 6
independent reading: and close reading, 124, 128; support for, 91–93, 105; texts for, 93t
individual tasks, 76t, 91–93
informational texts: analysis of, 12–13; purpose in, 53; readability formulas and, 36; structures in, 42–43
Innocenti, R., 56
instructional level, 6
instructional support, and challenging texts, 7–9, 14–16, 45–46
intimate language, 60
Ipcizade, C., 82
irony, 52t
Ivens, S.H., 23

J
Jenkins, L., 4
Jepsen, M., 5
Johnston, P., 7
Jones, C.F., 123
Joos, M., 59
journal writing, 126–127, 132
Jungeblut, A., 4
Just, M.A., 25
Justice, L.M., 78

K
Kafka, F., 45
Kane, M.J., 78
Kantor, R.N., 32
Kapur, M., 11, 89
Kelly, F.J., 6
Kesey, K., 57, 93
Killgallon, P.A., 7
Kintsch, W., 17, 24, 33, 43, 78
Kipling, R., 61, 106
Kirsch, I.S., 4
knowledge demands: in challenging texts, 48f, 60–65; examples of, 66–67; and text matching, 75t, 81–82
Kobayashi, M., 42
Koegel, T.J., 74
Kolstad, A., 4
Konigsburg, E.L., 86
Konopak, B.C., 42
Krampe, R.T., 81